The Windows Azure Handbook

Volume 1:
Planning & Strategy

David Pallmann

To my friends and colleagues at Neudesic, Microsoft, and the Windows Azure community

The Windows Azure Handbook, Volume 1: Planning & Strategy
David Pallmann
Foreword by Mickey Williams

ISBN-13: 978-1456574710
ISBN-10: 145657471X

TABLE OF CONTENTS

FOREWORD

When disruption in the business technology arena occurs, the change is often so drastic that it requires a completely new way of working in the new world order. Windows Azure is a new platform that certainly has the ability to change the way we solve business problems using technology—and it does so without making current skills obsolete. Although there is certainly a lot to learn about Azure, and this book is a great start, it's possible to be incredibly productive without discarding your existing investments in your development skills and tools. Azure is one of those rare technologies where we can effect great business change without completely changing technical direction.

I have a vivid recollection of when I first heard about Azure; or more accurately, the Microsoft project that would eventually be called Azure. It certainly sounded compelling, and several of us at Neudesic immediately considered it to be a fundamental change in the way that we would build applications. Fortunately for us, David Pallmann picked up the Cloud Computing ball and immediately began to run with it. Starting with our initial exposure to Microsoft's cloud platform, David has been a fountain of knowledge and inspiration for all things Azure. I don't think I've ever seen anyone in technology leadership so single-mindedly determined to learn as much as possible about a new platform, then exploit and disseminate that knowledge to others.

As we worked through the initial series of Windows Azure introductions and rollouts, David made the observation that the greatest need of prospective adopters was concrete information on planning. Among the many applications that David has built, his ROI calculator and assessment tool have been incredibly powerful (and popular). David has done all of us a great service by resisting the impulse to throw source code at us in his initial volume. While the need for programming guidance certainly exists, the need for planning and strategy is greater. Having said that, I look forward to the upcoming volumes; I also refer you to his excellent blog and his contributions on CodePlex, where a great deal of Azure-friendly source code exists.

Although this won't be the only book on Windows Azure, David has taken a few steps to make this book (and the series) more relevant. By publishing electronically, David has significantly shortened the amount of time required to bring the book to the community. As a side-effect, it's also very easy to release updates, and, without the market requirements from the dead-tree book-publishing world, he's free to publish volumes as they make sense technically, rather than satisfying some marketing need. He's not the first author to threaten to self-publish (raises hand), but he's the first author I know that has actually self-published a text so timely and useful. And I'm a hard grader.

This book is the first step in learning how to fully exploit the Windows Azure platform. Good luck in your development efforts and I look forward to seeing the reaction of the Azure community as this and future volumes are released.

Mickey Williams
Vice President, Technology Platform Group
Neudesic LLC

PREFACE

"He has his head in the clouds."
—Proverb

As I write this, I can truly say I have my head in the clouds: I am flying at 39,000 feet looking down over a blanket of cloud cover! I'm on my way to Europe to continue a multi-city training tour for Windows Azure, Microsoft's cloud computing platform. Fittingly, my plane's flight path takes us right over Dublin and Amsterdam—home of two Windows Azure data centers.

The view reminds me of the global nature and worldwide significance of cloud computing—and how much it has changed my world in just 2 years' time! The last year has been a blur, putting me in front of many audiences in many places for cloud computing assessments, Windows Azure training, and conferences. The technology—and the opportunity it brings—is exciting and I love sharing it. This book gives me another means of doing that.

Most books on cloud computing seem to be either *business-focused and general* or *deeply technical and platform-specific*. In my view, either level of focus is myopic: I'm a firm believer that when technology is applied both the business context and the technical context need to be jointly considered and in alignment. I also find the full lifecycle of cloud computing (planning, design, development, management) is rarely addressed in a single work. I see therefore a need and opportunity for a book series that tells the full story about cloud computing with Windows Azure.

I believe I'm in a unique position to tell that story well. As a Microsoft MVP I'm kept well-informed about where the platform is and where it is going and I'm exposed to industry thought leaders. As general manager of a consulting practice I and my colleagues are helping customers adopt cloud computing in the real world and are in tune with the best practices. My involvement in business activities such as cloud computing assessments has given me insight into the benefits, risks, and trade-offs companies must consider in evaluating and adopting cloud computing. My regular involvement in solution architecture and development allows me to speak about both from a position of hands-on experience. The big picture is a compelling one, and you'll get a good sense of it from this book.

I trust you will find *The Azure Handbook* helpful as you explore, evaluate, and adopt cloud computing with Windows Azure. I'm excited for what it can mean for you and your organization. Remember to keep your head in the clouds and your feet on the ground.

David Pallmann
February 2011

ACKNOWLEDGEMENTS

I couldn't have written this book without help. First, I'd like to thank Tim Marshall and Mickey Williams of Neudesic who both encouraged me to go deep on Windows Azure and made it possible for me to do so—for several years running now.

By all rights I should include a long list of Microsoft personnel here as well, but I don't want to increase this book's page count any further (or leave someone out). I'll simply say I am in debt to a great many Microsoft employees in the product groups and in the field, many of whom I consider to be friends and colleagues.

As excited as I was to publish my first "do-it-yourself, who-needs-a-publisher" book, I'm well aware that outside help in technical review and proofreading is an essential ingredient. I am very grateful to the following reviewers who reviewed chapters and pointed out opportunities for improvement in everything from technical accuracy to sentence structure: Maarten Balliauw (RealDolmen), Michael S. Collier (Centric Consulting), Jon Cortez (Neudesic), Yves Goeleven (Capgemini Belgium), Jason Milgram (Linxter), Parsa Rohani (Neudesic), Abhilash Shanmugan (Neudesic), Sathish TK (Neudesic), Kris van der Mast (Eandis), Bill Wilder (Fidelity Investments), Junao Xue (Push Management Consulting) and Bill Zack (Microsoft). Any remaining errors or omissions are of course my responsibility (please do check for errata at http://azurehandbook.com).

0

INTRODUCTION

"Oh! Clouds! Give me good advice."
—*Aristophanes, The Clouds, 419 B.C.*

This book is about *cloud computing* using Microsoft's *Windows Azure* platform. Accordingly, I have a two-fold mission in this introduction: to convince you cloud computing is worth exploring, and to convince you further that Windows Azure is worth exploring as your cloud computing platform. Following that I'll explain the scope, intended audience, and organization of the book.

WHY THE CLOUD?

First, let's talk about cloud computing in general. There are 3 things you should know about it: it's big, it's real, and it's exciting. You don't have to take my word for it: it's easy to try for yourself and most who do find the experience immediately addictive. So here's an up-front warning: cloud computing may ruin you for the traditional way of doing IT! Cloud computing has a great business story, a great technology story, and is personally empowering and satisfying to use. However, it's not appropriate for all uses and following a disciplined approach is essential in order to maximize benefit and avoid risk. That's where this book can help.

Cloud Computing is Big. When I say cloud computing is *big*, I mean it is a major technological wave transforming the very way we compute. That's not an over-statement: the computer industry is taking a hard look at refactoring everything we do in hardware, software, and networking for the better. That does mean some things in the cloud are different from in the enterprise, but the changes are usually not difficult to adapt to and can pay off in a big way financially and technically. Like virtualization, cloud computing's appeal is broad enough that just about every enterprise is expected to use it eventually in one way or another.

Cloud Computing is Real. When I say cloud computing is *real*, I mean there is something to it and that it is here to stay. While there is a lot of hype and misuse of the term "cloud" out there, cloud computing is nevertheless a real and tangible thing: an on-demand, service-based way to do computing—that comes with technical, financial, and operational implications. We can be quite specific about it and are in this book. Nor is cloud computing some sort of fad or trial balloon: it represents investments of billions of dollars by major technology providers and owes its roots to what the industry has learned about supporting large online communities with dynamic scale over the last 15 years.

Cloud Computing is Exciting. When I say cloud computing is *exciting*, I mean it has ignited a passion and buzz that's hard to ignore. You likely already have a sense of that: I'm writing this in early 2011 and you can't escape hearing about the cloud wherever you go even if you're not in technical circles. Why all the excitement? One reason is that the business and technical benefits are so significant—especially relevant in these recent times of economic upheaval. Another reason for excitement is the cloud fosters easy experimentation: it's never been easier for an entrepreneur to launch a start-up than with cloud computing, where there are no up-front IT costs other than developing your software. Yet another reason, cloud computing is still young and the rate of innovation is off the charts. It's very reminiscent of the early days of flight, or radio, or personal computing: chock full of opportunities for everyone. It's not just for the big players, as anyone can offer a new kind of cloud service and profit from it.

Cloud computing might sound similar to some past initiatives, many of which didn't succeed. Didn't the Application Service Provider (ASP) and Network Computer movements have similar aspirations? They did indeed, but their timing was wrong. Their undoing was the lack of a worldwide supporting infrastructure with the necessary virtualization technologies and elastic nature. The cloud isn't powered by the Internet; it's powered by sophisticated cloud computing data centers *accessed* via the Internet.

The cloud computing craze might be reminiscent in another way. If you recall the .com boom (and subsequent .com bust) perhaps you are wondering if we aren't on similar shaky ground here. That's a fair question to ask, but rest assured cloud computing has a different and far more solid foundation. Cloud computing's viability does not rest on numerous start-up companies with unproven profitability models asking Wall Street to invest. Rather, cloud computing is something that's been developed by established major technology providers, is already in use, has a well-defined business model, aligns strongly with today's business drivers, and has a ready-made market in the enterprise. Cloud computing isn't going to hurt the economy, it's helping us bounce back.

WHY MICROSOFT?

If this whets your appetite for cloud computing, the follow-up question is which platform to use? Let me give you some reasons to consider the Microsoft platform for cloud computing: breadth, symmetry, synergy, and experience.

Breadth. The *breadth* of the Microsoft cloud computing platform is vast. It includes subscription-based access to business and productivity applications in the cloud including CRM, Office, SharePoint, and Exchange. It includes Windows Azure, a platform for running your own business applications and the subject of this book. Services provided by Windows Azure go way beyond mere hosting and span compute (application hosting), relational data, storage, communication, security, networking, and synchronization services.

Symmetry. The Microsoft platform provides unique *symmetry* between enterprise and cloud. For decades Microsoft has provided technologies and products for the enterprise and now we are getting counterparts in the cloud. While it will take some time to fully match the enterprise stack in the cloud, we already have many products that exist in both places and feature gaps between them are being rapidly closed. This symmetry allows each organization to choose their preferred split between cloud and on-premise and adjust it over time as desired.

Synergy. If you have a large investment in Microsoft technology in the enterprise, you'll find a lot of *synergy* with the cloud. You can leverage your existing skills in Microsoft frameworks, languages, tools, and products such as the .NET Framework, ASP.NET, WCF, Silverlight, C#, T-SQL, Visual Studio, and SQL Server Management Studio. In addition, Microsoft is providing comprehensive support for other languages, development platforms, and tools—including Java, PHP, and the Eclipse IDE.

Experience. Microsoft has a great deal of *experience* providing online services. While the term cloud computing has only sprung into use recently, Microsoft has been supporting large online communities for 15+ years and handles billions of online transactions daily. In addition, Microsoft has been one of the biggest innovators in reinventing large data centers to support massive capacity with on-demand elastic scale and automated management.

SCOPE AND INTENDED AUDIENCE

The Windows Azure Handbook has an ambitious mission: to fully cover the capabilities of the Windows Azure platform and to equip you for the full lifecycle of using it. Accordingly, these books have business and technical content. You should get something valuable out of this series if you find yourself in any of these roles:

- Business Decision Maker
- Technical Decision Maker
- Architect
- Application Developer
- IT Operations Manager

Business topics include evaluating cloud computing, weighing risk vs. reward, the billing model, estimating TCO and ROI, and planning for cloud computing. You'll gain insights that will help you formulate a cloud computing strategy for your company and build a business case for moving your applications to the cloud.

Technical topics include features, architecture, development, and management. While you'll find plenty of technical content, both theoretical and practical, I've made no attempt to exhaustively document the Windows Azure APIs: the documentation is readily available online, the platform is fast-moving, and the broad scope of this book series doesn't leave room for every last technical detail. I've focused instead on conveying and illustrating the capabilities and characteristics of the platform; the paradigms and patterns for software design; and the basics and best practices for implementation, including migration of existing applications.

The content is organized into sections for each role, making it easy to go directly to the area that interests you. For those who will read the series end to end, the volumes are arranged in an orderly sequence based on lifecycle that begins with business justification and ends with operations monitoring.

ORGANIZATION

The *Windows Azure Handbook* is a 4-volume series:

- Volume 1: Planning & Strategy
- Volume 2: Architecture
- Volume 3: Development
- Volume 4: Management

Volume 1 (the book you're holding) is concerned with understanding, evaluating, and planning for the Windows Azure platform. Here's how it's organized:

Part 1, *Understanding Windows Azure*, acquaints you with the platform and what it can do.

- Chapter 1 explains cloud computing.
- Chapter 2 provides an overview of the Windows Azure platform.
- Chapter 3 describes the billing model and rates.

Part 2, *Planning for Windows Azure*, explains how to evaluate and plan for Windows Azure.

- Chapter 4 describes a responsible process for cloud computing evaluation and adoption.
- Chapter 5 describes how to lead discussions on envisioning risk vs. reward.
- Chapter 6 is about identifying cloud opportunities for your organization.
- Chapter 7 explains how to profile applications and determine their suitability for Windows Azure.
- Chapter 8 describes how to approach migrations and estimate their cost.
- Chapter 9 covers how to compute Total Cost of Ownership (TCO) and Return on Investment (ROI).
- Chapter 10 is about strategies for adopting Windows Azure.

GOALS

Every writer learns from their publishing experiences and seeks to improve the next time around. This is my fourth book, and I have some specific goals:

1. **Brevity over Verbosity**. 'Nuff said!
2. **Handbook.** I've long wanted to write a "handbook" or field guide, the spirit of which is to synthesize into one volume the essential information you would otherwise find only by consulting many individual sources.
3. **Self-Published**. I am self-publishing this book through Amazon.com's CreateSpace service rather than using a traditional book publisher. This is an interesting experiment and I'm attracted to the autonomy this approach gives authors to do things their way. It seems fitting that a book about on-demand computing should use on-demand publishing!
4. **E-Book and Print Editions**. This book can be ordered as a print book or an e-book, another first for me. This acknowledges the trend toward digital content and electronic book readers without forsaking the availability of an in-hand, bound volume which some prefer.
5. **Timing**. Several of my past books have been victims of what turned out to be poor timing for their subject matter, coming out too early or too late. This time, I think the timing is just right. Windows Azure has just

had its one year anniversary of commercial availability and a host of exciting new features have just been released. I'm expecting *The Windows Azure Handbook* will be the first Azure book out that covers the new wave of platform features.

TERMINOLOGY

Writers have to make terminology decisions. Here are some choices I've made:

AppFabric

"Windows Azure Platform AppFabric" is a mouthful! I've saved some trees and gone with "AppFabric" for brevity. There's also potential to confuse Windows Azure AppFabric with Windows Server AppFabric. Unless otherwise specified, any use of AppFabric should be understood to mean the Windows Azure version.

Capitalization of Design Pattern Names

In Volume 2: Architecture, the architectural chapters include design pattern catalogs. In these areas only I've followed a common design pattern convention to capitalize the names of design patterns in the text.

URL vs. URI

"A URL is a URI but not all URIs are URLs." Volumes 2 and 3 use these terms quite a bit. In the majority of places where you see "URI" or "URL", either term could have been used. I suppose the safest thing would have been to just use URI everywhere but I find that reads awkwardly at times and so I've used the terms that seem most natural based on what is being discussed.

Windows Azure vs. Cloud

I'll sometimes refer to Windows Azure specifically and other times simply say "cloud" or "cloud computing". There are 2 reasons for this. First, some of the things that are true of Windows Azure are generally true of cloud computing. Second, it gives brevity and keeps every tenth word in the manuscript from being "Windows Azure".

Windows Azure / Windows Azure Platform

"Windows Azure" is both the name of the platform and one of its feature areas (Windows Azure, SQL Azure, and AppFabric). When it isn't completely obvious from the context, I say "Windows Azure platform" when discussing the platform.

SUPPORT

The companion site to this book is AzureHandbook.com, and I also invite you to visit AzureDesignPatterns.com and AzureSamples.com. Any book corrections will be posted on AzureHandbook.com. To download companion book content, you'll need this download key: 145657471X. The companion content for Volume 1 is primarily planning worksheets.

AzureDesignPatterns.com provides an online design patterns catalog that complements Volume 2: Architecture.

AzureSamples.com links you to all of the online Windows Azure code samples I am aware of.

I write about the Windows Azure platform frequently on my blog at http://davidpallmann.blogspot.com. I can be contacted through my blog site or by email at dpallmann@hotmail.com.

Time is the enemy of all technical books. This first edition of *The Windows Azure Handbook* reflects the state of the Windows Azure platform, version 1.3, as of February 2011. The passing of time will surely bring new platform services. It could also bring changes to the platform's architecture, programming model, or pricing model. You can get the most current information about the platform at Azure.com.

GET STARTED!

Do yourself and your company a big favor and look into cloud computing and Windows Azure. You'll be glad you did! This book will show you how.

PART 1
UNDERSTANDING
WINDOWS AZURE

CLOUD COMPUTING EXPLAINED

"What is it? Pray tell me."
—*Aristophanes, The Clouds, 419 B.C.*

In order to appreciate the Windows Azure platform it's necessary to start with an understanding of the overall cloud computing space. This chapter provides general background information on cloud computing. We'll answer these questions:

- What is cloud computing?
- How is cloud computing being used?
- What are the benefits of cloud computing?
- What different kinds of cloud computing are there?
- What does cloud computing mean for IT?

CLOUD COMPUTING IN A NUTSHELL

Around the world, cloud computing is transforming organizations—often in very different ways—and having a financial, technical, cultural, or strategic impact. Here are some examples of how the cloud is making a difference:

- A maker of desktop publishing software moves into the 21st century by offering publishing as a print-on-demand online service.
  Cloud computing can transform your business model and means of delivery.
- A web site for automotive reference data uses cloud computing to handle overflow when peak demand exceeds the capacity of their data center.
  Cloud computing gives you capacity on tap you don't pay for until used.
- A tax preparation service uses cloud computing to obtain hefty amounts of computing power during tax season.
  Cloud computing is elastic, allowing you to expand / reduce deployment as needed.
- A company moves their global web site from traditional hosting to cloud computing. Their hosting costs drop from $150K a year to $50K.
  Cloud computing can dramatically reduce your IT costs.
- A hurricane relief fund uses cloud computing for their web site. They're unsure how long they will keep the site going and need flexibility of term. They can stay in the cloud as long as they need to, or walk away any time.
  Cloud computing gives you the flexibility of not committing to a term of use.
- An animation company renders movie frames on server farms in the cloud. For each rendering job users can choose between allocating new servers (for faster completion) or using existing servers (for lessened expense).
  Cloud computing gives you choices allowing you to balance capacity vs. expense.
- A company whose end of month processes used to take 24 hours on a local server can now do the work in 1 hour by briefly renting 24 cloud servers.
  Cloud computing opens new styles of computing to you such as burst computing.

- A large church uses cloud computing to back up their membership and giving records, which are safely archived in the cloud with triple redundancy. *Cloud computing is a safe place to keep your data.*

- A financial services start-up runs all of their IT in the cloud; their only on-premise equipment is laptops. *Cloud computing allows you to outsource some or all of your IT.*

- A large retailer coordinates with its supply chain through the cloud, federating dozens of security providers and communicating across the firewalls, NATs, and proxies of multiple companies. *Windows Azure federates security and communication across organizations.*

- A business in a developing nation is able to compete more effectively because cloud computing gives them access to the world's finest data centers. *Cloud computing levels the IT playing field for countries, companies, and individuals around the world.*

As you can see from these examples, there are many different ways to take advantage of cloud computing and businesses of all kinds and sizes can benefit. Those who stereotype cloud computing as only being fit for one particular use or scenario are doing themselves a disservice.

Cloud Computing is a Style of Computing

The first and most important thing to know about cloud computing is that it is a *style* of computing. There's interesting technology involved to be sure but it's the style of computing that's at the heart of things. If we compare standard computing to buying a home with a 30-year mortgage, cloud computing is like renting an apartment month-to-month—with the option to upgrade, downgrade, or leave at any time with guaranteed availability and no hassles when you terminate. We call this freedom to expand or reduce your usage at will *elasticity*. Cloud computing is all about flexibility.

That flexibility, and the manner in which it is delivered, translates to serious efficiency. This efficiency is manifested in several ways, one of which is *cost efficiency*. Computing from a cloud computing data center typically costs less than in the enterprise. Reduced costs come from the use of shared resources and the economy of scale and reduced energy costs found in cloud computing data centers. In addition, you only pay for resources while you need them, releasing them the moment you're through with them. You're never wasting an IT dollar with cloud computing. Once you're using cloud computing at a significant level, you can also expect reduced labor costs since many management functions are automated for you.

Cloud computing also brings you *operational efficiency*. You can allocate servers and deploy software to the cloud in minutes—about 20 minutes in the case of the Windows Azure platform. Compare that to the traditional amount of time it takes to procure, configure, and deploy servers in your organization, which might be anywhere from 6 weeks to 6 months. Not only are these activities faster in the cloud, they're fully automated and there's no one in line ahead of you: the inevitable bottlenecks that form in enterprise IT and the resulting need to prioritize some projects over others are happily absent from the cloud computing experience.

While cloud computing is relatively new by that name, it's also been a long time in coming. The influence of past forms of computing is apparent such as timesharing. Many movements of the past, even if never fully realized, helped pave the trail to where we are today including the notions of Application Service Providers and the Network Computer. The technologies that make cloud computing possible derive from the growing sophistication of data centers that support vast online communities and massive scale. Chief among these are advances in virtualization.

Just Like Electricity

I've found the easiest way to explain cloud computing succinctly is to make the analogy to utility services such as electricity. You already understand electricity, and as you'll see this goes a long way toward understanding what cloud computing is like.

Computing is going the way of electricity

Do you own a home generator? Most of you reading this do not, preferring to trust in the availability of your local electricity provider. Even if you do have your own way to generate power locally, it's very likely you only use it for emergencies. The vast majority of us plug into the wall for our electrical needs on a day-to-day basis.

What's good about this model? Lots of things! First of all it's *easy*: you just plug into the wall and your device starts working. It's also *ubiquitous*: wall outlets are to be found everywhere you go. Your usage is metered and *billing is consumption-based*: you only pay for what you use, and only use what you need. Lastly, there's plenty of *capacity on tap*: you can use 10 times as much electricity this month as you did last month without having to do anything formal like notifying the utility or renegotiating a contract. You simply draw more power and you'll have an accordingly larger bill. Similarly, you can use less power next month and will have a smaller bill without incurring any kind of penalty. Utility service is a good model, and it's exactly where computing is going.

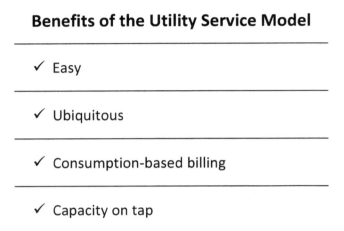

Benefits of the Utility Service Model

✓ Easy

✓ Ubiquitous

✓ Consumption-based billing

✓ Capacity on tap

The utility service model is hard to beat. We like it for our electrical service, our water service, our phone service, and our fuel services. Now we can compute that way too.

On-Demand Computing

Cloud computing data centers allocate resources on demand. When you need IT assets such as virtual servers or storage, you simply request them online and minutes later you have them. There's no advance notice required, no up-front purchasing of servers, no term or usage commitments, and no waiting. The figure below illustrates an initial deployment where 2 virtual servers are allocated. Your monthly bill will reflect charges for servers, storage, and bandwidth.

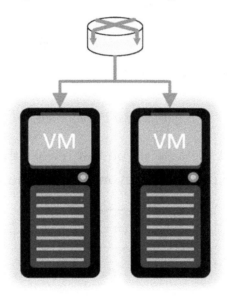

On-Demand Deployment

Over time, you may decide you need to expand your deployment in response to growing demand. Again this is a simple matter of requesting the increase online and receiving it minutes later. The next figure below shows the deployment being increased from 2 servers to 3. This increases your capacity and of course your monthly bill. Similarly, you could reduce your deployment if you saw demand decrease which would lower your bill.

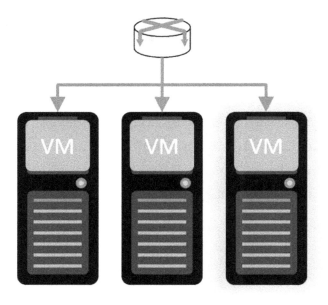

Expanding a Deployment

When you no longer need the assets, you can release them altogether. You won't have any legal or financial obligation beyond the current month's bill.

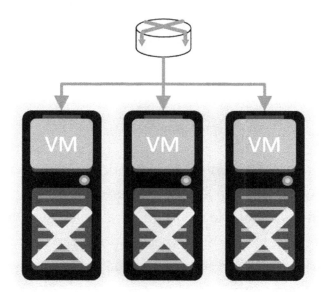

Removing a Deployment

Sophisticated Infrastructure, Commodity Hardware

Cloud computing data centers have extremely sophisticated infrastructure. They can dynamically allocate (or release) mammoth amounts of resources on demand in just minutes. They allow shared use of resources while keeping tenants safely isolated from each other.

Despite the sophisticated infrastructure, cloud computing data centers use average, commodity hardware in order to keep costs low. This means occasional hardware failure is to be expected. Cloud computing data centers combat failure through redundancy. Redundant VMs keep your application available in the face of a server failure. Redundant storage keeps your data intact in the face of a drive failure. These redundant resources are spread across different areas of the data center to prevent a catastrophic failure from affecting all instances of a resource.

Cloud Computing Myths and Misconceptions

There are plenty of misconceptions about cloud computing. Let's clear them up.

Myth: Cloud computing is nothing but hype / is not real / has no meaning or definition.
This is simply not so. Cloud computing is definable, real, and very significant.

Myth: Cloud computing just means accessing applications over the Internet.
This common but incorrect belief misses the point entirely: cloud computing is all about the new breed of elastic data centers and the services they make possible. The Internet is merely the fabric for connecting users and devices to cloud services.

Myth: Cloud computing is only appropriate for large-scale applications.
Cloud computing makes plenty of sense for organizations of all sizes.

Myth: Cloud computing automatically adjusts your deployment size based on usage.
This is *sometimes* true but not all cloud computing platforms and services have this characteristic today. Many cloud services are adjusted manually.

Myth: Cloud computing is another name for grid computing.
They are *not* the same thing—grid computing predates cloud computing by over a decade and has its own semantics—but they do share some common characteristics such as massive parallelism. Grid computing on top of a cloud computing infrastructure makes tons of sense.

Myth: Cloud computing locks you in to a vendor.
This is only true to the extent you want it to be true. If you architect your applications to strongly leverage a cloud platform and take advantage of unique capabilities, you won't be able to run it somewhere else without making modifications. On the other hand it's perfectly feasible to write applications that stick to what's common between cloud and enterprise and remain portable. The choice is yours.

Myth: Cloud computing gives you high-end hardware.
Cloud computing data centers do not generally provide high-end or high-performance hardware. They use average, commodity hardware which is what keeps costs low.

Types of Cloud Computing

There are 3 generally accepted categories of cloud computing: SaaS, PaaS, and IaaS. The experience is quite different at each level, so getting acquainted with them to inform your decision-making is strongly recommended. Once you are using cloud computing for more than one purpose you might find yourself using more than one of these.

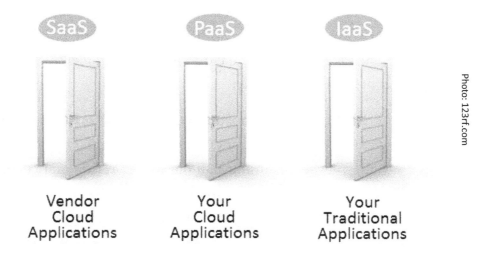

SaaS, PaaS, and IaaS

- *Software-as-a-Service* (SaaS) is where you make use of packaged software in the cloud, applications you pay for through subscription models. For example, a CRM system in the cloud whose monthly cost is based on the number of users. You don't typically have any visibility into the architecture or implementation details of SaaS applications; you simply *use* them.

Most SaaS applications are *multi-tenant*, meaning they are serving you as well as other corporate clients from a single deployment. This requires the vendor to keep tenant data isolated and protected. The SaaS application may or may not permit you to customize its behavior, something the multi-tenancy aspect makes difficult for vendors.

SaaS gives you access to *vendor cloud applications*.

- *Platform-as-a-Service* (PaaS) is where you subscribe to a platform on which you can host your own business applications and data. For example, hosting your business web site in the cloud and making use of cloud services for compute, database and security.

PaaS is different from simply hosting your applications: the services provided are virtualized, scalable, and managed for you. For example, a data storage service may seem similar to a file server at first glance, but the storage service protects your data with redundant copies, provides automatic failover, and can serve up content over the Internet through a global delivery network. That's a lot of value for pennies per gigabyte per month.

Fully leveraging PaaS may mean some changes from how you do things in the enterprise but this should not scare you away from it. For migration of existing applications, you'll likely want to keep changes to a minimum for cost reasons. Applications written for farms or that follow the principles of Service-Oriented Architecture (SOA) are particularly easy to move to the cloud. For new applications, architecting with the cloud platform in mind will take maximum advantage of what it has to offer; alternatively you can choose to emphasize portability and limit yourself to features found both in the cloud and in the enterprise.

PaaS is for *your cloud-oriented applications*.

- *Infrastructure-as-a-Service* (IaaS) is where you have access to [virtualized] hardware such as servers or storage devices and can control them directly at a low level. For example, creating a VM image that contains your business application and hosting it on servers in the cloud.

  IaaS isn't much different from traditional hosting except that you can easily add or remove instances and aren't locked in to a long-term arrangement. While some view IaaS as the easiest way to get started with the cloud, it puts the burdens of reliability, maintenance, and management on you. You also need to ensure your data is safely persisted to guard against failures.

  IaaS is for *your traditional, self-managed applications.*

The SaaS and PaaS categories strongly leverage the benefits of cloud computing whereas IaaS gives up some of them such as automated management. Where does Windows Azure fit into this categorization? Primarily at the PaaS level. Windows Azure is a platform you can use to put your own applications in the cloud. There is also some IaaS capability but PaaS is considered to be the high road.

The lines between SaaS, PaaS, and IaaS are starting to become blurred. For example, a CRM service in the cloud is normally thought of in the SaaS category but many CRMs can be considered application platforms in their own right, putting them in the PaaS category as well. As enterprises start to make use of cloud computing more heavily we can expect to see more and more composite solutions that combine elements of SaaS, PaaS, and IaaS.

Which cloud computing door should you go through? If you're planning on using packaged software from a vendor who offers it in the form of an online subscription service, you'll be using SaaS. For running your own applications in the cloud, you need to decide between PaaS and IaaS.

IaaS vs. PaaS

The table below contrasts some of the differences between the IaaS and PaaS approaches. IaaS may look attractive at first glance because you don't need to make your application "cloud enabled" and it may seem more familiar to your IT people if they've used traditional hosting. However, you are taking on a lot of management responsibility for yourself including software installation, configuration, licensing, and patching. In particular, you should be aware that the persistence of VM instances is not guaranteed (at the time of this writing). That means a VM's disk is not a safe place to keep long-term data and limits the suitable scenarios.

The PaaS approach is superior because you receive an environment managed for you and are using a platform whose services are inherently scalable and protected through redundancy and failover mechanisms. In addition, the PaaS approach gives you access to the full services of your cloud platform which likely include valuable new capabilities that are out of reach of traditional applications.

PaaS	IaaS
Applications must target cloud platform (designed for cloud or migrated to cloud).	Traditional application may be able to run unmodified in the cloud.
Software environment, licensing, and maintenance are provided for you.	Software environment, licensing, and maintenance are your responsibility.
You can take advantage of compute elasticity (adding, removing instances).	You may or may not be able to run in a multiple instance configuration.
You can leverage cloud data services with redundancy & reliability protections.	Enterprise data paradigms may be single points of failure in the cloud.
Persistence of data is achieved through platform services.	Persistence of data is your responsibility.
The cloud platform may offer you new capabilities not found in the enterprise.	You are limited to common ground between enterprise and cloud.

To illustrate the difference between the PaaS and IaaS approach, let's imagine you have a simple web site that uses a back-end database and you want to move the entire solution into the cloud. The figure below illustrates the difference between the IaaS and PaaS architectures.

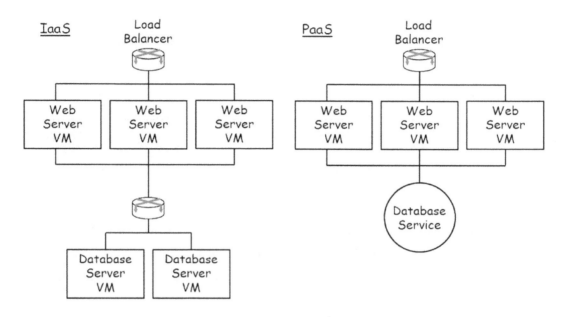

Example of IaaS vs. PaaS

With the IaaS approach, you'd likely set up one VM farm for the web site and another VM farm for the database. In the cloud, you'd upload your VM, allocate instances, configure your front end farm to point to your database farm, and start your instances running. Web traffic to your front-end VMs is load-balanced across your instances by the cloud environment.

Now let's compare that to the PaaS approach. You package and upload your web application to the cloud, allocate one or more instances, configure your front end to point to a cloud database service, and start your instances running. Web traffic to your front-end VMs is load-balanced across instances by the cloud environment.

In this comparison you can see that there's a lot of similarity on the web site tier—both use a farm of VM instances to host an application—but the database tier is handled very differently. As the figure above shows, we escape the need for back-end VM(s) for the database in the PaaS approach because we are instead using a database *service*. That saves us the work of installing and configuring and managing a database server, the cost of licensing a database product and hosting it, and the work of setting up a server cluster to avoid having a single point of failure.

There's a big danger to the IaaS approach that needs to be pointed out: generally, the cloud computing provider won't guarantee the persistence of your VM instances. That means if you're running a database server product in a VM or VM farm you could lose your local disk. When you instead use a cloud service outside of your farm, you get persistence.

There are other, less apparent differences. Over time, the PaaS approach is going to keep you up to date with the latest operating system, patches, and database software. In the IaaS model, you must first of all pay license fees for the software you use and you're solely responsible for maintenance and upgrades.

Services Provided by Cloud Computing

Many people associate cloud computing with *hosting*—executing applications in a cloud computing data center. However, a "compute service" is only one of many kinds of services cloud computing can provide. Cloud services do almost everything under the sun, from storing data to managing virtual networks. The specific services available vary between platforms and this is one way in which cloud vendors compete.

The table below compares the services available from Google App Engine, Amazon Web Services, and Windows Azure as of February 2011. Some disclaimers are in order. In looking at this comparison, keep a few things in mind:

- Cloud computing is a fast-moving area. Additional services are always appearing so this shouldn't be considered an exhaustive comparison.
- When platforms offer services in the same category they are not necessarily equal in functional scope, value, or pricing model.
- Some of these services are in the preview stage and are not yet commercially released.
- These core services are only a starting point since other companies offer additional cloud services for each platform.

Services Provided by Leading Cloud Computing Platforms

	Google AppEngine	Amazon Web Services	Microsoft Windows Azure
Compute Service	AppEngine	Amazon EC2	Windows Azure Compute
Storage Service	GFS, Chubby, BigTable	Amazon S3	Windows Azure Storage
Relational Database Service	Hosted SQL	Amazon RDS	SQL Azure Database
Reference Data Service	Public Data Explorer		DataMarket
Reporting Service			SQL Azure Reporting
Virtual Network Service		Amazon VPC	Windows Azure Connect
Security Service	OAuth Service	Identity and Access Management (IAM)	AppFabric ACS
Communication Service		Amazon SNS	AppFabric Service Bus
Cache Service	Memcache Service		AppFabric Cache
Monitoring Service		Amazon CloudWatch	Diagnostics API
Management Service		Amazon CloudWatch	Service Management API
Content Delivery Service		Amazon Cloud-Front	Windows Azure CDN
Payment Service		Amazon FPS	

Email Service	Mail Service	
Image Processing Service	Image Service	
Scheduling service	Cron Service	
Distributed computing of large data sets	Google MapReduce	Amazon Elastic MapReduce

How are these services set up and accessed? Enabling and configuring services is usually accomplished interactively through an online management portal but may also be automatable from program code or scripting. For compute (hosting) services, the process typically involves uploading some kind of application package or VM image to the management portal, allocating VM instances, and starting them running. You're then consuming the service on an ongoing basis, according to its metering rules, until you put a stop to it.

Aside from compute services, most cloud services are consumed via HTTP REST calls. In some cases, a cloud service will support a different protocol than REST that is more native to its purpose. For example, Microsoft's SQL Azure Database service speaks TDS, the same protocol used by SQL Server, for compatibility reasons.

THE BENEFITS OF CLOUD COMPUTING

Cloud computing provides many benefits. Chief among them are these:

- Reduced cost: save over doing IT on-premise or with traditional hosting
- Convert capital expenditures (CapEx) to operating expenditures (OpEx)
- Consumption-based pricing: only use what you need, pay for what you use
- Elasticity: expand or reduce the size of your deployments any time
- Scale: lots of capacity on tap
- No commitment: no obligation beyond the current month's bill
- Faster Time to Market: rapid deployment of new / upgraded software
- Management: automated management simplifies IT and saves on labor

We'll be more specific about benefits in Chapter 2 as we talk about the Windows Azure platform in particular.

Challenges Facing Today's Enterprise

Many enterprises are facing one or more of the challenges listed below. Cloud computing can materially help with each of them.

Challenges Facing Today's Enterprise

Challenge	How Cloud Computing Helps
Pressure to Reduce Costs	• Lowered IT costs • Consumption-based pricing • Labor savings
Control Costs Better	• Replace server purchases and upgrades with a monthly pay-as-you-go bill • Only pay for resources while needed • Convert CapEx to OpEx
Data Center Planning	• Handle any load even if unanticipated • Reserve capacity without paying till needed • Augment with cloud rather than expanding your data center • Build for average load rather than peak load • Alternate location for disaster recovery
Continue to Provide Full / Expanding Services	• Leverage automated management • Simplify IT / Self-service IT
Need for Increased Agility	• Fast time to market • Elasticity • Easy entry / easy exit • Do away with server procurement cycle • No waiting in line behind other IT projects
Barriers to Innovation	• Do away with server purchases / CapEx approvals • New capabilities / gain a competitive edge • Outsource some IT & focus on your business

Pressure to Reduce Costs

Every business today has pressure to reduce costs. Cloud computing can bring about reduced IT costs for most businesses, and the level of savings is dramatic for some organizations. With consumption-based pricing you only pay for what you use and only use what you need. If you adopt cloud computing at a significant level, you can also expect to save on labor costs because some management tasks previously performed by IT staff are now being done automatically.

Need to Control Costs Better

Cost control is just as important as cost reduction. In the cloud, your spending is much smoother because you are converting capital expenditures (buying equipment) to operating expenditures (paying for a service). Those expensive budget hits for up-front server purchases (and periodic upgrades) are replaced by a pay-as-you-go monthly bill. You only pay for resources while you need them. For many companies this means a healthier balance sheet and fewer barriers to getting new projects underway.

Data Center Planning

Your data center may be nearing its limits or your future capacity needs may be unclear. Your budget for expanding or upgrading your data center may have been slashed, reallocated, or deferred. You can lean on the cloud to pick up the slack. The capacity is there to handle any change in load even if unanticipated; yet you're not paying to reserve this capacity and charges only apply when you actually use it. As an alternative to expanding your data center you can use the cloud to augment what you already have. This raises the interesting idea of sizing your data center to target average load rather than peak load.

Maintain Full/Expanded Services

Despite the financial climate and related challenges you're probably expected to continue providing full IT services—perhaps even expanded services to support new capabilities that are in demand such as mobility—and probably without any increase in staff or budget. You can outsource some of your IT work to the cloud and take advantage of automated management. You can also democratize IT, making more IT functions available to your employees for self-service.

Need for Increased Agility

Most businesses could use an improvement in agility. The cloud offers you many capabilities that can help you become more nimble. You can get software and updates to market quickly with cloud deployment, bypassing the lengthy procurement and provisioning cycle. The cloud's elasticity allows you to allocate, expand, reduce, or remove a deployment in minutes. You can easily enter or exit use of the cloud without complications. Many of the bottlenecks that are inevitable within the enterprise simply don't apply in the cloud because you're not waiting in line behind other projects with higher priorities.

Barriers to Innovation

Businesses need to innovate in order to compete but there are often barriers to innovation such as being able to gain budget approval for new hardware capital expenditures. With the cloud these up-front costs vanish and are replaced with easier-to-accommodate monthly operating expenditures. Depending on the cloud platform, you may find new capabilities that allow you to innovate ranging from new business models such as SaaS to new technical features such as federated security services. Cloud computing allows you to focus more on your business and less on IT.

Cost Efficiency of Consumption-based Pricing

The cost efficiency of cloud computing can be significant to your bottom line. You no longer have to buy servers in advance and go through refresh cycles every couple of years, relieving your budget from periodic bursts of spending. Accordingly you no longer have to try to predict your exact peak load and hope you have enough servers in place; in the cloud you can simply adjust up and down based on the load you're seeing.

The two figures that follow illustrate the difference. The first figure on the next page depicts IT spending in the enterprise. The jagged line represents hypothetical load on an application over time. Load goes up at times, down at times. The staircase pattern shows what we do in the enterprise: we buy hardware (the vertical part of the line), then time goes by (the horizontal part of the line), then we repeat. We buy more hardware because we are seeing demand increase or expect it to increase. If demand goes up too steeply and we can't respond in time, we have an under-supply of capacity. When demand goes down, we have more capacity on hand than is needed, a wasteful excess of supply.

This is completely what we're used to, but it's far from ideal. You're spending more money than you have to or spending it earlier than you have to.

Let's compare this to IT spending in the cloud, where you have a monthly pay-as-you-go bill and no large outlays for hardware. The second figure shows the same hypothetical application load. In the cloud, you simply watch your load and adjust the size of your deployment in the cloud to closely match. You can see how much more efficient this is.

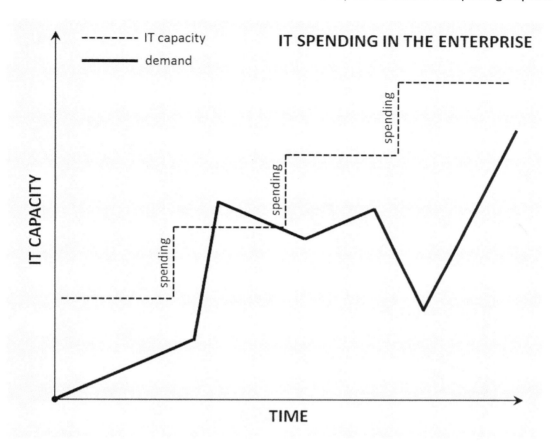

IT Spending In the Enterprise

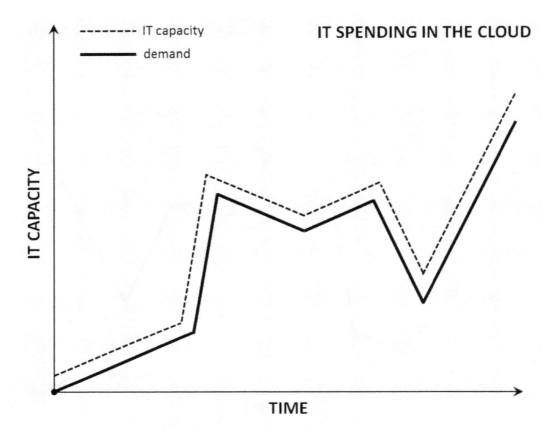

IT Spending in the Cloud

Strong Scenarios for Cloud Computing

Some application scenarios are a strong fit for cloud computing. Getting familiar with them can help point the way to your best candidates for the cloud. Often the "low hanging fruit" cloud opportunities (those that bring the greatest return and are the most straightforward to move) are in these application categories.

Scenario	Why Suitable
Public-facing Web Sites	Public-facing web sites in your perimeter network (DMZ) are usually an easy move to the cloud. You're already comfortable with this application being on the Internet. Moving it to the cloud should present a minimum of controversy.
Apps with Changing Load	Applications whose load varies benefit from cost efficiency. You're only paying for resources while you need them.
Apps with an Uncertain Lifetime	In the cloud you have easy entry and easy exit.
Apps that Need to Scale Fast or Fail Fast	For entrepreneurial / startup scenarios, the cloud is the best place to experiment. If you are successful you can stay in the cloud as long as you want and go as big as you want. If you fail, you can pull the plug and walk away cleanly.
Data Center Extension	If your data center is near its limit, moving existing or new applications to the cloud can be an alternative to investing in a larger data center. If your data center is generally adequate but you need to handle overflow during peak periods, the cloud can be used to extend capacity.
Disaster Recovery	If you need an off-site place to back up data or fail over to in the event of a catastrophe, the cloud can be that location.
SaaS Business Model	If you're interested in taking advantage of the SaaS model for your own applications, the cloud is the ideal place to do SaaS.

Strong Scenarios for Cloud Computing

Usage patterns alone can justify a move to the cloud if they have an interesting enough shape. Where there is increase, decrease, cycles, fluctuation, or on-off changes in load the cost efficiency of the cloud becomes very attractive. This is not to say that flat, unchanging load is necessarily a bad fit for the cloud but other considerations need to be looked at.

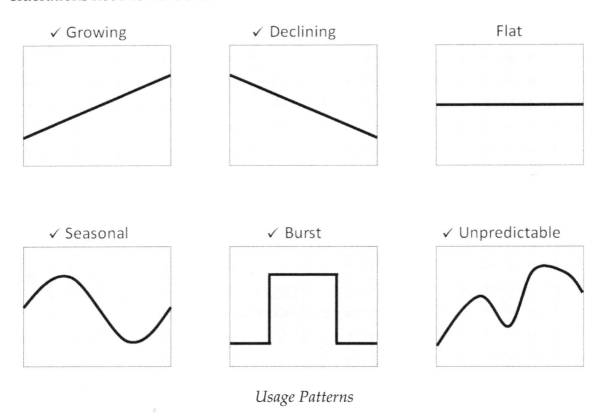

Usage Patterns

Uncertainty Favors the Cloud

One of the most interesting and unique things about cloud computing is that the more *uncertainty* you have the stronger the cloud's appeal is. Are you unsure of the longevity of your application? Cloud computing makes sense because you can exit anytime. Will the load on your application fluctuate, or are you uncertain of what the usage profile will be? Cloud computing is the safe move: all the capacity you might need is there, but you only pay for what you actually use and can go larger or smaller anytime. The flexibility this gives you cannot be overstated: you no longer have to plan your IT needs years in advance and hope you have accurately predicted them. In recent times where there has been a lot of uncertainly, cloud computing is a breath of fresh air.

WHAT THE CLOUD MEANS FOR IT

IT departments often have conflicted feelings about cloud computing, feeling torn. On the one hand, the potential benefits are highly attractive and cloud computing may already be on senior management's radar. On the other hand, cloud computing can raise anxiety and uncertainty in the minds of IT people about what the impact will be on the company, on their department, and on staff.

A Negative Scenario

If you're in the IT department, you may be suspicious that cloud computing might bring some or all of the following upon you:

- New and untrusted ways of doing things
- A loss of control
- A loss of security
- Putting corporate assets at risk
- Making IT's job harder than ever
- Pressure from the business to adopt before IT is ready
- Uncontrolled use of the cloud throughout the organization
- IT department becoming less relevant

That's certainly a dark picture! —but not the way it has to be at all. There may be some level of validity to these concerns but they are overblown as stated and can be avoided. Especially since most established companies are not going to move *all* of their IT to the cloud. Before anyone goes jumping off of bridges, let's examine another outcome.

A Positive Scenario

Cloud computing can be a very positive development for an IT department. It can mean all of the following:

- A trusted complement to your data center (trust earned incrementally)
- The luxury of extra capacity at a moment's notice
- Efficient use of IT dollars lets you do more with less
- Managed use of cloud and enterprise leverages the best of each
- IT freed up to focus on the strategic use of technology
- IT leads the way in the organization's use of the cloud
- Democratization of IT across the company (guided by the IT department)
- IT department more relevant than ever

That's a much rosier picture, isn't it? What determines the outcome more than anything else is the response of the IT department to cloud computing.

The Risk of Waiting on the Cloud

Because cloud computing is a self-service technology it is also an invasive and disruptive one. IT departments ignore it at their peril. We're already hearing stories where some employee became an instant hero by doing themselves, with $200 and a credit card, what IT could not or would not do for them. If you're in IT, episodes like this should signal to you that there's a need to participate in cloud computing adoption. Avoiding or ignoring cloud computing will not prevent it from coming. Instead it will simply happen around you, uncontrolled and uncoordinated. There are risks associated with that.

The Opportunity for IT

The opportunity for IT is to embrace cloud computing and guide its evaluation, adoption, and management within the company. IT can play a key role in the financial and technical evaluation of cloud computing, in formulating strategy and policies for its use, and in managing cloud computing production assets.

Will cloud computing change your job? Yes, probably. There will likely be some functions you'll no longer need to provide as often, such as procuring and configuring servers; but there will also be new services you will need to provide, such as managing your assets in the cloud. A DBA may no longer need to worry about the physical management of databases but they will still be very much needed for the logical part of their jobs.

CHAPTER SUMMARY

In this chapter we introduced the phenomenon of cloud computing, a style of computing that revolves around elastic on-demand IT resources and consumption-based pricing. We used examples to illustrate the diversity of cloud computing, and made an analogy to electrical service to illustrate the utility characteristics of cloud computing.

We also looked into the benefits of cloud computing, which include reduced costs, flexibility without commitment, increased organizational agility, and faster time to market. We saw how cloud computing helps meet the challenges faced by many organizations today and examined scenarios that are a strong fit for the cloud.

Finally, we discussed what cloud computing can mean for IT, pointing out the outcome of cloud computing adoption is very much dependent on IT's response to the cloud. We ended with an appeal for IT departments to lead the way in bringing cloud computing into their organizations rather than avoiding or opposing it.

2

WINDOWS AZURE
PLATFORM OVERVIEW

"Go where he will, the wise man is at home,
His hearth the earth, his hall the azure dome."
—from Woodnotes, Ralph Waldo Emerson, 1847

In the previous chapter we explained cloud computing generally. Now it's time to get specific about the Windows Azure platform. We'll answer these questions:

- Where does Windows Azure fit in the cloud computing landscape?
- What can Windows Azure do?
- What are the technical underpinnings of Windows Azure?
- What are the business benefits of Windows Azure?
- What does Windows Azure cost?
- How is Windows Azure managed?

MICROSOFT CLOUD COMPUTING

Cloud computing is one of those "bet the company" strategic moves for Microsoft that affects the entire organization. Externally, that commitment is evidenced by a comprehensive set of cloud offerings whose capabilities range from business and productivity applications in the cloud to a platform for putting your own applications in the cloud. Internally, it is evidenced by Microsoft moving more and more of its own online properties and systems into cloud computing environments. Make no mistake, cloud computing is transformational at Microsoft.

Microsoft has been operating online services for over 15 years, and the company stated in 2010 that it supports over 200 cloud services, 1 billion customers, and 20 million businesses in over 76 markets worldwide—including more than 500 state and local governments in 48 U.S. states.

Microsoft Cloud Services

Microsoft has an enormous line-up of online services that span from Bing to Xbox LIVE. For brevity purposes we're going to focus on the subset of those services that are formally marketed as cloud computing services. Microsoft's cloud offerings are grouped into 2 overall service categories, *Microsoft Online Services* (SaaS) and the *Windows Azure Platform* (PaaS/IaaS).

Microsoft Online Services

Microsoft Online Services are cloud-hosted editions of Microsoft business and productivity applications. Chief among these are CRM Online and Office 365 (formerly known as BPOS).

CRM Online is a cloud-hosted equivalent to the Microsoft Dynamics CRM enterprise product. It provides relationship tracking and helps with sales workflow, marketing campaigns, and customer service. CRM Online is sold as a SaaS subscription service where your monthly charges are based on the number of users.

Office 365, the successor to BPOS, bundles multiple productivity applications hosted in the cloud including Microsoft Office, Microsoft Office Web Applications, SharePoint Online, Exchange Online, and Lync (Office Communicator and Live Meeting). Office 365 is sold as a SaaS subscription service where your monthly charges are based on the number of users and the package you select (which determines which applications are included). Office 365 provides Single Sign-on and unified web-based administration.

Microsoft Online Services

Offering	Category	Description
CRM Online	SaaS	Cloud-hosted Microsoft Dynamics CRM
Office 365	SaaS	Cloud-hosted productivity apps bundle
Office Web Apps	SaaS	Cloud-hosted Office
Exchange Online	SaaS	Cloud-hosted Exchange
SharePoint Online	SaaS	Cloud-hosted SharePoint
Lync	SaaS	Cloud-hosted Lync (Office Communications and Live Meeting)

Windows Azure Platform

The Windows Azure Platform is Microsoft's platform for hosting your own applications in the cloud. It can be used at both the PaaS and IaaS level, but PaaS is highly preferred and encouraged. Since applications come in many shapes and sizes, there are multiple services in Windows Azure in order to provide a full set of building blocks. They include compute (hosting), storage, network, relational database, communication, and security functionality and more are being added all the time. These services are grouped under 3 primary functional areas, named Windows Azure, SQL Azure, and AppFabric.

Windows Azure Platform

Offering	Category	Description
Windows Azure	PaaS, IaaS	Core cloud services
SQL Azure	PaaS	Relational data cloud services
AppFabric	PaaS	Enterprise-strength cloud services

Whereas the Microsoft SaaS offerings have simple pricing models based on number of users, Windows Azure platform pricing is based on which services you use, and each service has its own metering rationale.

Microsoft Data Centers

Cloud computing would be nowhere without the right back end infrastructure. When we say an application runs "out there in the cloud", we mean the application and data are hosted in a cloud computing data center.

Global Infrastructure

Microsoft is currently operating 6 Windows Azure data centers around the world and more have been announced. As this map shows, these data centers are located in San Antonio Texas, Chicago Illinois, Dublin Ireland, Amsterdam Netherlands, Hong Kong, and Singapore. Cloud computing data centers are allocated based on Internet traffic density rather than trying to equilaterally cover the globe.

Windows Azure Data Centers

Map: Wikimedia Commons

These cloud computing data centers are the anchors of the worldwide infrastructure but there are additional elements. One of them is a global network of 24+ edge servers that form a content delivery network.

Data Center Architecture

A Windows Azure data center has a radically different design from a traditional data center. In place of a building with large server rooms containing raised floors and endless racks of equipment, the data center consists of modular, self-contained units, pre-assembled and delivered to the data center ready for use. These units are capable of sitting outdoors, so it isn't even necessary for a data center to have a roof. The Chicago-area data center is over 17 football fields in size and boasts over 300,000 servers.

These modular units, called *containers*, are formally known as IT Pre-Assembled Components (ITPACs). A container (illustrated below) is extremely self-contained. Externally, only 3 connections are needed, for air, power, and coolant. Inside a container are framing, flooring, server racks, a transformer, a control panel, partitions, fans, exhaust dampers, bus bars, servers, lights, mixing dampers, air washers, intake louvers, filters, and a skin. Containers come in a few different form factors. They can hold hundreds or thousands of compute servers and draw energy in the range of 200 to 600 kilowatts. The newer generations of containers don't require fans: ambient air is drawn over a membrane where water is being slowly released, cooling the air by 20-25 degrees.

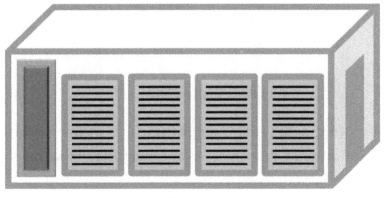

Container

Containers are the unit of management in the data center. When equipment failures in a container reach a certain threshold, tenant traffic is relocated and the container is taken out of service.

If you're interested in how the internal components of a container are arranged, there's a Microsoft video on the subject online at http://www.microsoft.com/showcase/en/us/details/84f44749-1343-4467-8012-9c70ef77981c.

Data Center Security

Microsoft protects its infrastructure and data centers against physical intrusion. Facilities use industry-standard access mechanisms, and access is limited to a small number of operations personnel who are required to regularly change their access credentials. Data center access and approval authority are tightly controlled. When data center equipment has reached the end of its life, strict processes are followed for data handling and hardware disposal.

Network protections include firewalls, gateways, intrusion detection systems, and a redundant internal and external DNS infrastructure with restricted write access. Tenants of the data center are fully isolated from each other.

These protections and others are described in the Microsoft White Paper, *Windows Azure Security Overview*, available at http://www.microsoft.com/windowsazure/-whitepapers/papers/default.aspx.

THE WINDOWS AZURE PLATFORM

In case you're wondering about the name, Azure (pronounced AH'zure) is a shade of blue (from a French word meaning, ironically, "the color of a cloudless sky").

Major Feature Areas

The Windows Azure platform has many services, grouped into 3 functional areas: Windows Azure, SQL Azure, and AppFabric. Each area is described in further detail later in this chapter.

Windows Azure Platform

Functional Area	Category	Services Provided
Windows Azure	PaaS, IaaS	• Compute service • Storage service • Content delivery network • Virtual network service • DataMarket service
SQL Azure	PaaS	• Database service • Reporting service • Database sync service • Database access service
AppFabric	PaaS	• Access control service • Service bus (communication service) • Cache service

Note that one of these functional areas is named "Windows Azure" but the entire platform is also named "Windows Azure". The best way to avoid confusion is to refer to the platform as "Windows Azure Platform".

Another potential cause of name confusion is the name "AppFabric": there are two offerings from Microsoft with this name, Windows Azure AppFabric and Windows Server AppFabric. They will converge over time but today they have differing features. Since this book is about Windows Azure, any mention of AppFabric should be taken to mean Windows Azure AppFabric unless stated otherwise.

Benefits of the Windows Azure Platform

Windows Azure provides many business and technical benefits, listed below. In addition to the common benefits of cloud computing, Windows Azure is noteworthy for its breadth of capabilities and the level of management it provides.

Windows Azure Benefits

Area	Benefits
Financial	• Reduced cost
	• Convert capital expenditures (CapEx) to operational (OpEx)
	• On-demand computing - only pay for resources while needed
	• Metered service and consumption-based pricing
	• Labor cost savings from automated management
Agility & Flexibility	• Faster time to market – rapid provisioning and deployment
	• Ease of entry / ease of exit

	• Elasticity – expand or reduce deployments whenever desired
	• No term or usage commitment on your part
Scale & Reliability	• Capacity on tap
	• High availability via server redundancy
	• Data reliability via storage redundancy
	• Service Level Agreement (SLA) aids business continuity
Accessibility	• Broadly accessible global infrastructure
	• Enabler of mobility / multi-device support
Streamline IT	• Self-service IT empowers departments and employees
	• Simplify IT
	• Automated management
Transform IT Culture	• Outsource aspects of IT
	• Focus on your business not IT
	• Eliminate bottlenecks
	• Frees up internal resources for other things
	• For new businesses, enables Zero IT
	• Enables new styles of computing such as burst computing
Innovation	• Provides new technical capabilities
	• May enable new business models for your organization

	• Levels the playing field for smaller companies and nations
Eco-friendly	• Green data centers are designed for eco-friendliness
	• Shared tenants use less energy than they would individually
Technical superiority	• Better and simpler refactoring of application architecture
	• Promotes principles of Service-Oriented Architecture (SOA)
	• Decouples service delivery from application implementation

Management and The Fabric

Management is a key differentiator between the Windows Azure platform and other cloud computing platforms. The "cloud operating system" for Windows Azure is called *the Fabric*. The Fabric carries out management tasks such as allocating and deallocating resources and deploying software. It also monitors your applications for health and carries out recovery operations. The Fabric keeps your virtual machines up to date and safe by applying patches and software updates.

Case Studies

In the previous chapter we gave many examples of how businesses are leveraging cloud computing. You might be interested in some concrete examples of how the Windows Azure platform is being put to use and by whom. You can find over 150 Windows Azure case studies online at http://www.microsoft.com/windowsazure-/evidence/. You can browse or search case studies by company, technology, benefit obtained, industry, or country.

Managing Windows Azure

Billing Account and Billing Portal

To work with Windows Azure you need to set up a billing account with the Microsoft Online Customer Portal at https://mocp.microsoftonline.com. From this portal you can also view and manage your bills.

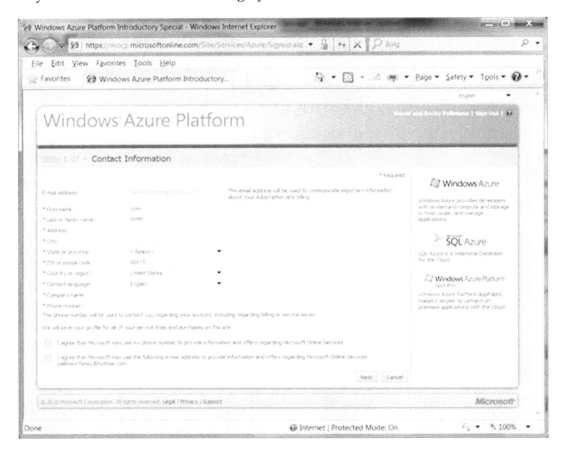

Microsoft Online Customer Portal

The pricing model and use of the billing portal are described in Chapter 3, *Billing*.

Windows Azure Portal

Your Windows Azure account is managed through the use of a portal which you can access at http://windows.azure.com. From the portal you create projects, allocate and manage resources, and deploy software.

The portal is often referred to as the "Windows Azure Developer Portal" by Microsoft but it's certainly not for developers only, since IT professionals will use this portal to deploy and manage production solutions. In fact it's very important that you use separate accounts for development and production to avoid accidents from affecting production, just as you would do in the enterprise.

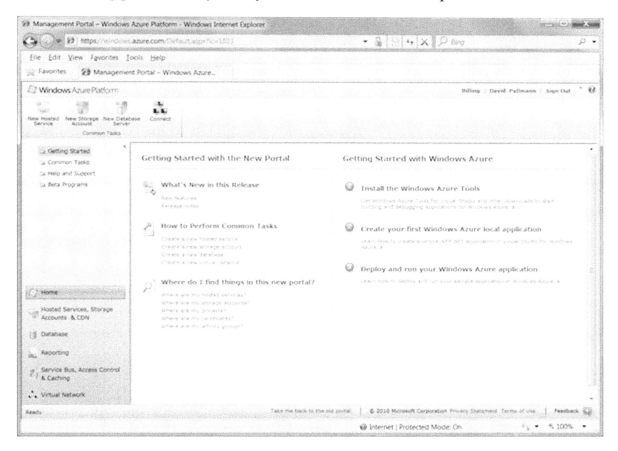

Windows Azure Portal

For detailed use of the portal refer to Volume 3 (Development) and Volume 4 (Management) of The *Windows Azure Handbook*.

Developing for Windows Azure

Microsoft seeks to provide developers with a familiar development experience in the Windows Azure platform, allowing them to use their preferred language, development platform, and tools. Volume 3 of *The Windows Azure Handbook* goes into detail about the developer experience.

Development with Microsoft Technologies and Tools

Developers who work regularly with Microsoft tools, languages, and technologies will find it very easy to start working with Windows Azure:

- The *Windows Azure Software Development Kit (SDK) and Tools for Visual Studio*, downloadable from Azure.com, adds templates to Visual Studio and installs a local simulation environment.
- Database tools such as SQL Server Management Studio can be used with the SQL Azure database.
- The .NET Framework (version 3.5 or later) and technologies such as ASP.NET, Silverlight, and WCF can be used with Windows Azure.

You're not restricted to .NET managed code and languages like C# and VB.NET with Windows Azure. Native applications such as those developed in C++ can also run on the platform.

Other Development Platforms and Tools

Microsoft wants developers from all corners to be able to the use the Windows Azure platform. That includes Java, PHP, and Ruby developers. There are SDKs and accelerators that target those development platforms available which include integration with the Eclipse IDE. You can find out more about Windows Azure platform interoperability at http://azure.com/interop.

Windows Azure Simulation Environment

Windows Azure provides a local cloud simulator that developers can use to develop and test locally on their own machines before deploying to the cloud. The simulator gives developers the ability to do a certain amount of their development and testing without incurring billing charges and without the need to be connected to the Internet.

Currently, the simulation environment simulates Windows Azure Compute (hosting) and Windows Azure Storage. In addition, SQL Server or SQL Server Express can be used to simulate the SQL Azure Database service locally. There is no local simulation environment currently available for other platform services.

WINDOWS AZURE: CORE SERVICES

The Windows Azure area of the platform includes many core services you will use nearly every time you make use of the cloud, such as application hosting and basic storage. Currently, Windows Azure provides these services:

- Compute Service: application hosting
- Storage Service: non-database storage
- CDN Service: content delivery network
- Windows Azure Connect: virtual networking
- DataMarket: marketplace for buying or selling reference data

Windows Azure Compute Service

The Compute service allows you to host your applications in a cloud data center, providing virtual machines on which to execute and a controlled, managed environment. Windows Azure Compute is different from all of the other platform services: your application doesn't merely consume the service, it runs in the service.

The most common type of applications to host in the cloud are Internet-oriented, such as web sites and web services, but it's possible to host other kinds of applications such as batch processes and middleware. You choose the size of virtual machine and the number of instances, which can be freely changed.

Windows Azure
Compute Service

YOUR
APPLICATION
HOSTED

Here's an example of how you might use the Windows Azure Compute Service. Let's say you have a public-facing ASP.NET web site that you currently host in your enterprise's perimeter network (DMZ). You determine that moving the application to the Windows Azure platform has some desirable benefits such as reduced cost. You update your application code to be compatible with the Windows Azure Compute Service, requiring only minor changes. You initially update and test the solution locally using the Windows Azure Simulation Environment. When you are ready for formal testing, you deploy the solution to a staging area of the

Windows Azure data center nearest you. When you are satisfied the application is ready, you promote it to a production area of the data center and take it live.

Windows Azure Storage Service

The Storage service provides you with persistent non-database storage. This storage is external to your farm of VM instances (which can come and go). Data you write is safely stored with triple redundancy, and synchronization and failover are completely automatic and not visible to you.

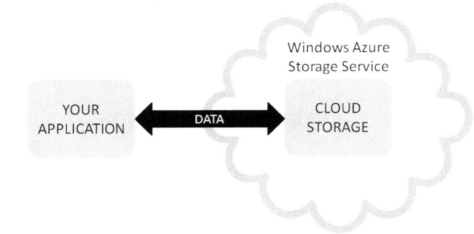

Windows Azure Storage provides you with 3 kinds of storage: blobs, queues, and tables. Each of these has a rough counterpart in the enterprise: blobs are similar to files, queues are similar to enterprise queues, and tables are similar to random-access data files or simple database tables (there are no relational database features). In each case however there are important differences to be aware of. All 3 types of storage can scale to a huge level; for example a blob can be as large as 1 terabyte in size and a table can hold billions of records.

Windows Azure Storage Types

Storage Type	Description	Example use
Blob Storage	Similar to file storage	Store images for your web site
Queue Storage	Similar to enterprise queues	Store orders needing fulfillment
Table Storage	Similar to random-access data files	Store contact records

Blobs can be made accessible as Internet URLs which makes it possible for them to be referenced by web sites or Silverlight applications. This is useful for dynamic content such as images, video, and downloadable files. This use of blobs can be augmented with the Windows Azure CDN service for global high-performance caching based on user locale.

Here's an example of how you might use the Windows Azure Storage service. You have a cloud-hosted web site that needs to serve up images of real estate properties. You principally keep property information in a database but put property images in Windows Azure blob storage. Your web pages reference the images from blob storage.

Windows Azure CDN Service

The Content Delivery Network (CDN) service provides high performance distribution of content through a global network of edge servers and caching. The CDN has about 24 edge servers worldwide currently and is being regularly expanded.

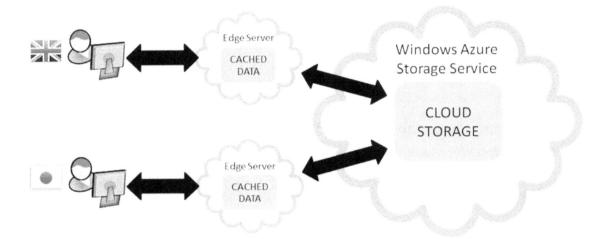

A scenario for which you might consider using the CDN is a web site that serves up images, audio, or video that is accessed across a large geography. For example, a hotel chain web site could use the CDN for images and videos of its properties and amenities.

As of this writing, the CDN service currently serves up blob storage only but additional capabilities are on the way. At the PDC 2010 conference, Microsoft announced new CDN features planned for 2011 including dynamic content caching, secure SSL/TLS channels, and expansion of the edge server network. Dynamic content caching in particular is of interest because it will allow your application to create content on the fly that can be distributed through the CDN, a feature found in many other CDN services.

Windows Azure Connect

Windows Azure Connect provides virtual networking capability, allowing you to link your cloud and on-premise IT assets with VPN technology, often referred to as *hybrid cloud*. You can also join your virtual machines in the cloud to your domain, making them subject to its policies. Many scenarios that might otherwise be a poor fit for cloud computing become feasible with virtual networking.

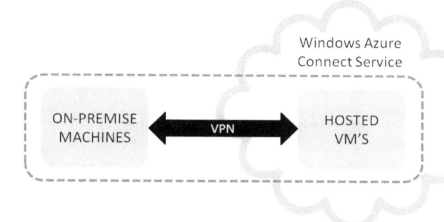

Here's an example of how you might use Windows Azure Connect. Suppose you have a web application you want to host in the cloud, but the application depends on a database server you cannot move off-premise. Using Windows Azure Connect, the web site in the cloud can still access the on-premise database server.

AVAILABILITY: At the time of this writing, this service is not yet released commercially but is available for technical preview.

Windows Azure Marketplace DataMarket

The Windows Azure Marketplace is an online marketplace where you can find (or advertise) partners, solutions, and data. In the case of data, the marketplace is also a platform service you can access called DataMarket. You can explore DataMarket interactively at http://datamarket.azure.com.

The DataMarket service allows you to subscribe to reference data. The cost of this data varies and some data is free of charge. There are open-ended subscriptions and subscriptions limited to a certain number of transactions. You can also sell your own reference data through the DataMarket service. You are in control of the data, pricing, and terms.

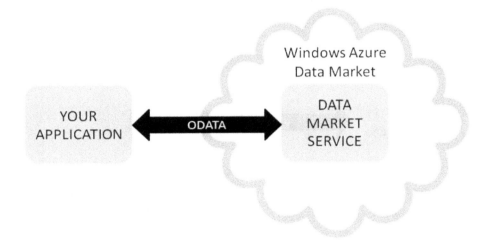

The data you subscribe to is accessed in an interoperable way using OData, a standard based on AtomPub, HTTP, and JSON. Because the data is standardized, it is easy to mash up and feed to visualization programs.

Here's an example of how you might use the DataMarket service. Suppose you generate marketing campaign materials on a regular basis and wish to customize the content for a neighborhood's predominant income level and language. You subscribe to demographic data from the DataMarket service that lets you retrieve this information based on postal code.

SQL Azure: Relational Data Services

The SQL Azure area of the platform includes services for working with relational data. Currently, SQL Azure provides these services:

- SQL Azure Database: relational database
- SQL Azure Reporting: database reporting
- SQL Azure Data Sync: database synchronization
- SQL Azure OData Service: data access service

SQL Azure Database

The SQL Azure Database provides core database functionality. SQL Azure is very similar to SQL Server to work with and leverages the same skills, tools, and programming model, including SQL Server Management Studio, T-SQL, and stored procedures.

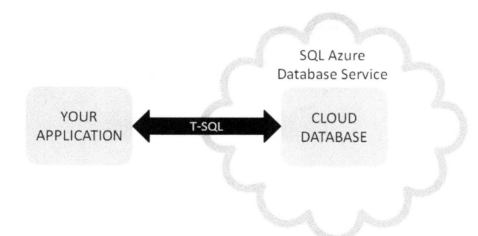

With SQL Azure, physical management is taken care of for you: you don't have to configure and manage a cluster of database servers, and your data is protected through replicated copies.

Here's an example of how you might use SQL Azure Database. You have a locally-hosted web site and SQL Server database and conclude it makes better sense in the cloud. You convert the web site to a Windows Azure Compute service and the database to a SQL Azure database. Now both the application and its database are in the cloud side-by-side.

SQL Azure Reporting

SQL Azure Reporting provides reporting services for SQL Azure databases in the same way SQL Server Reporting Services does for SQL Server databases. Like SSRS, you create reports in Business Intelligence Development Studio and they can be visualized in web pages.

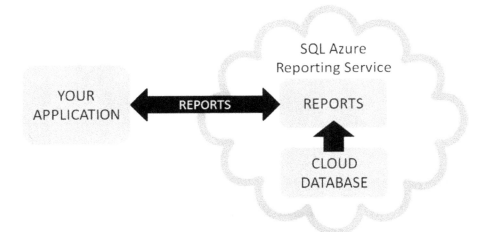

Here's an example of how you might use SQL Azure Reporting. You've traditionally been using SQL Server databases and SQL Server Reporting Services but are now starting to also use SQL Azure databases in the cloud. For reporting against your SQL Azure databases, the SQL Azure Reporting service is the logical choice.

AVAILABILITY: At the time of this writing, this service is not yet released commercially but is available for technical preview.

SQL Azure Data Sync Service

The SQL Azure Data Sync service synchronizes databases, bi-directionally. One use for this service is to synchronize between an on-premise SQL Server database and an in-cloud SQL Azure database. Another use is to keep multiple SQL Azure databases in sync, even if they are in different data center locations.

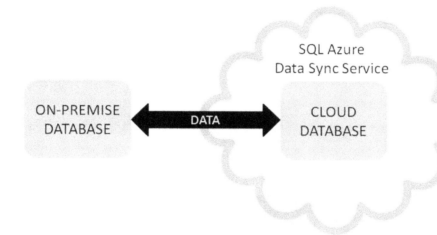

Here's an example of how you might use the SQL Azure Data Sync service. You need to create a data warehouse that consolidates information that is sourced from multiple SQL Server databases belonging to multiple branch offices. You decide SQL Azure is a good neutral place to put the data warehouse. Using SQL Azure Data Sync you keep the data warehouse in sync with its source databases.

AVAILABILITY: At the time of this writing, this service is not yet released commercially but is available for technical preview.

SQL Azure OData Service

The SQL Azure OData service is a data access service: it allows applications to query and update SQL Azure databases. You can use the OData service instead of developing and hosting your own web service for data access.

OData is an emerging protocol that allows both querying and updating of data over the web; it is highly interoperable because it is based on the HTTP, REST, AtomPub, and JSON standards. OData can be easily consumed by web, mobile, and desktop applications.

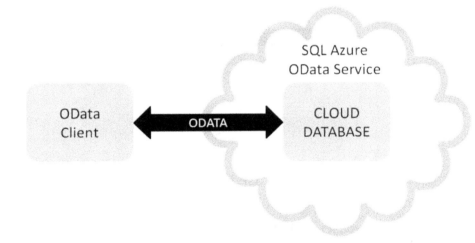

Here's an example of how you might use the SQL Azure OData service. Let's say you have data in a SQL Azure database that you wish to access from both a web site and a mobile device. You consider that you could create and host a custom web service in the cloud for data access but realize you can avoid that work by using the SQL Azure OData service instead.

AVAILABILITY: At the time of this writing, this service is not yet released commercially but is available for technical preview.

AppFabric: Enterprise Services

The Windows Azure AppFabric area of the platform provides enterprise-grade services and facilitates business-to-business scenarios. Currently, AppFabric provides these services for performance, communication, and security:

- AppFabric Access Control Service: federated security
- AppFabric Cache Service: distributed memory cache
- AppFabric Service Bus: publish-subscribe communication

In addition, several valuable AppFabric services are in development that you should watch for in the future:

- AppFabric Composition Service: a service and tooling for composing, deploying, and managing end-to-end applications on the Windows Azure platform.
- AppFabric Integration Service: an integration service with capabilities similar to what BizTalk Server provides (pipelines, transforms, adapters).

AppFabric Cache Service

The Cache service is a distributed memory cache. Using it, applications can improve performance by keeping session state or application data in memory. This service is a cloud analogue to Windows Server AppFabric Caching for the enterprise (code-named Velocity) and has the same programming model.

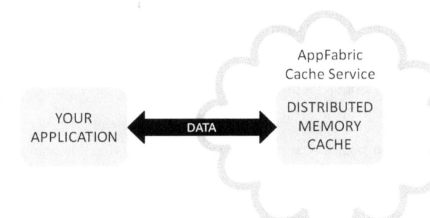

Here's an example of using the AppFabric Cache service. An online store must retrieve product information as it is used by customers, but in practice some products are more popular than others. Using the Cache service to keep frequently-accessed products in memory improves performance significantly.

AVAILABILITY: At the time of this writing, this service is not yet released commercially but is available for technical preview.

AppFabric Service Bus

The Service Bus uses the cloud as a relay for communication, supporting publish-subscribe conversations that can have multiple senders and receivers. Uses for the service bus range from general communication between programs to connecting up software components that normally have no way of reaching each other. The Service Bus supports traditional client-server style communication as well as multicasting.

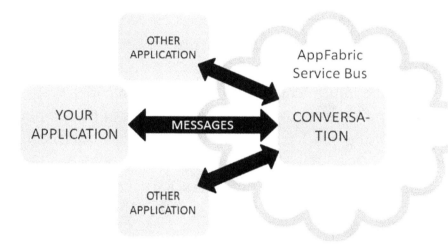

The Service Bus is adept at traversing firewalls, NATs, and proxies which makes it particularly useful for business-to-business scenarios. All communication looks like outgoing port 80 browser traffic so IT departments don't need to perform any special configuration such as opening up a port; it just works. The Service Bus can be secured with the AppFabric Access Control Service.

Here's an example of how you might use the Service Bus. You and your supply chain partners want to share information about forecasted and actual production activity with each other. Using the Service Bus, each party can publish event notification messages to all of the other parties.

AppFabric Access Control Service

The Access Control Service is a federated security service. It allows you to support a diverse and expanding number of identity schemes without having to implement them individually in your code. For example, your web site could allow users to sign in with their preferred Google, Yahoo!, Facebook, or Live ID identities. The ACS also supports domain security through federated identity servers such as ADFS, allowing cloud-hosted applications to authenticate enterprise users.

The ACS uses claims-based security and supports modern security protocols and artifacts such as SAML and SWT. Windows Azure applications typically use Windows Identity Foundation to interact with the ACS. The ACS decouples your application code from the implementation of a particular identity system. Instead, your application just talks to the ACS and the ACS in turn talks to one or more identity providers. This approach allows you to change or expand identify providers without having to change application code. You use rules to normalize the claims from different identity providers into one scheme your application expects.

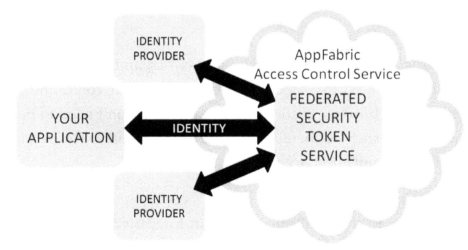

Here's an example of how you might use the ACS. Your manufacturing company has corporate clients across the country who need to interact with your online ordering, support, and repair systems—but you don't want the burden of administering each of their employees as users. With the ACS, each client can authenticate using their preferred, existing identity scheme. One customer authenticates with their Active Directory, another uses IBM Tivoli, another uses Yahoo! identities. Claims from these identity providers are normalized into one scheme which is all your applications have to support.

CHAPTER SUMMARY

In this chapter we shared what Microsoft is doing in cloud computing and where Windows Azure fits into the picture as a platform for running your own applications in the cloud. We learned about the capabilities and modular organization of the global network of Windows Azure data centers and supporting infrastructure. We reviewed the benefits, management experience, and developer experience of the platform and where online case studies can be found.

We also took a tour of the Windows Azure platform and its 3 primary functional groupings, each of which contains multiple services. Windows Azure provides core services for hosting, storage, virtual networking, and reference data. SQL Azure provides relational data services for database, reporting, synchronization, and data access. AppFabric provides enterprise-class services for federated security, firewall-friendly communication, and distributed memory caching. The Windows Azure platform is ever on the move, with newer services often available for preview prior to commercial launch.

3

BILLING

"Why so large a cost, having so short a lease, does thou upon your fading mansion spend?"
—William Shakespeare, Sonnet CXLVI, circa 1599

The Windows Azure platform has many capabilities and benefits, but what does it cost? In this chapter we'll review the billing model and rates. We'll answer these questions:

- How is a Windows Azure billing account set up and viewed?
- Is Windows Azure available in my country, currency, and language?
- What is the Windows Azure pricing model?
- What are the metering rules for each service?
- What is meant by "Hidden Costs in the Cloud"?

BILLING ACCOUNTS

Except for local development and testing, you will need a billing account in order to work with Windows Azure. There are various offers by which you may get some free hours before billing kicks in. Check the packages in the *Pricing* section of Azure.com to review the latest offers. If you have an MSDN subscription, it may entitle you to some free use.

Eventually, you will need to start paying to use the Windows Azure platform. This is usually done by setting up a billing account for credit card payment. It is also possible to set up invoicing terms. Your billing account is tied to a Live ID and will contain one or more *subscriptions*. Each subscription is subject to monthly billing if you make use of platform services. If you use the platform for more than one purpose you may find it useful to organize your billing into multiple subscriptions for easier tracking.

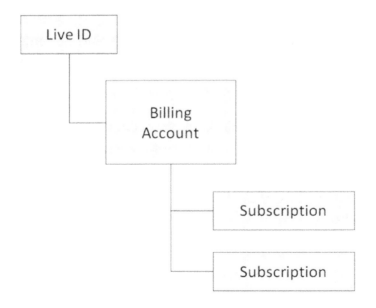

Relationship of Live ID, Billing Account, and Subscriptions

Setting up a Billing Account

To set up a billing account, sign in to Azure.com with a Live ID account you wish to use for identification. Go to the Purchase section of the site, review the available offers, and select one. You will be taken to the Microsoft Online Customer Portal where you can set up an account and a payment method.

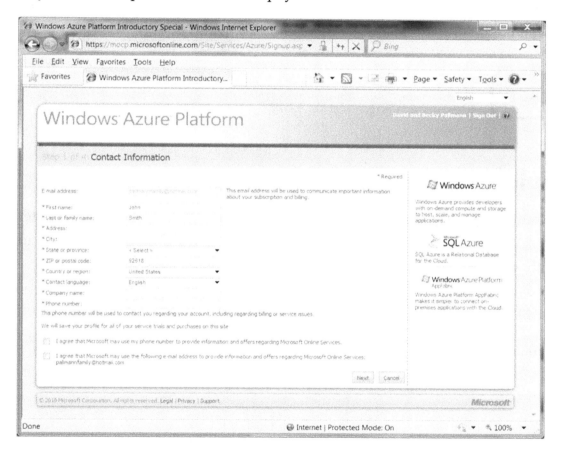

Microsoft Online Customer Portal

You'll return to this portal at https://mocp.microsoftonline.com whenever you wish to take a peek at your current or past bills. With cloud computing you'll want to get in the habit of regularly examining and managing your billing, just as a home consumer does with their utility bills. This is the best way to identity any unexpected trends in billing early on.

The billing portal is a separate web property from the Windows Azure portal but you can get to it easily. There is a *Billing* link at the top right of the Azure portal.

Reviewing Your Billing

The billing portal allows you to view your billing. You can view complete past bills and you can also view your accumulated charges to date for the current month, as shown in the example below. You'll see charges for each service area you're using, such as Windows Azure, SQL Azure, and AppFabric. Furthermore, you can drill into each charge line item to see usage details as shown below.

TIP: You can check your accumulating charges any time in the billing portal.

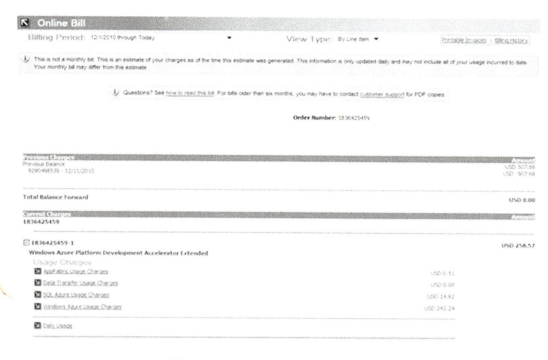

Viewing Monthly Billing Charges

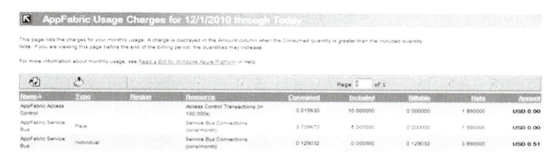

Viewing Charge Details

Country, Currency, & Language

Although the examples in this book are in U.S. dollars, Windows Azure is commercially available in these 41 countries as of this writing: Austria, Belgium, Canada, Denmark, Finland, France, Germany, Ireland, India, Italy, Japan, Netherlands, New Zealand, Norway, Portugal, Singapore, Spain, Sweden, Switzerland, UK, United States, Australia, Brazil, Chile, Colombia, Costa Rica, Cyprus, Czech Republic, Greece, Hong Kong, Hungary, Israel, Luxemburg, Malaysia, Mexico, Peru, Philippines, Poland, Puerto Rico, Romania, and Trinidad and Tobago.

If you cannot directly purchase Windows Azure from your home country you may want to investigate whether you can make purchase arrangements from one of the above countries if it is legal to do so. More countries may be added over time so always check the latest information at Azure.com.

Windows Azure online web sites are country-aware and adjust currency accordingly as described below. However, these sites are English-language only.

Setting Country in Azure.com

In the Azure.com web site you can set your country through a link at the top right. Pricing information is shown based on your country setting.

Setting Location in the Billing Portal

In the Microsoft Online Customer Portal (billing portal) you can set your location but this must be done <u>before</u> signing in.

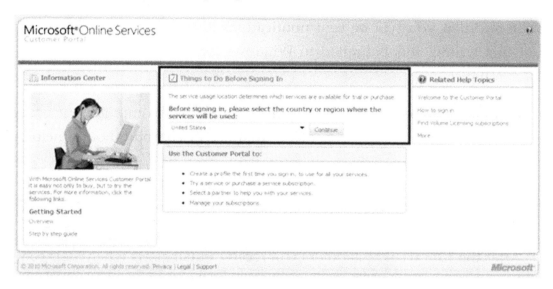

Notifications

The Windows Azure platform billing system will send you email notifications when a billing cycle completes (though you can inspect your charges-to-date anytime). In addition you will be sent notifications about your usage levels. At the time of this writing this is limited to Windows Azure Compute hours only and works as follows:

- Customers are sent email notifications when their compute hour usage exceeds 75%, 100% and 125% of the number of compute hours included in their plan.
- Customers on the standard consumption offer will receive email alerts every week with their compute hour usage for the previous week, for the first 13 weeks of their subscription.
- After the 13th week, customers will receive email alerts when their compute hour usage exceeds 75%, 100% and 125% of their monthly usage based on a three-month rolling average.

Here's an example email notification about usage level (partial):

Dear David Pallmann,

This e-mail notification comes to you as a courtesy to update you on your Windows Azure platform usage. Our records indicate that your subscription has exceeded 75% of the compute hours amount included with your offer for your current billing period. Any hours in excess of the amount included with your offer will be charged at standard rates.

Please see below for the amounts used to-date during your current billing period:

Subscription start date: 5/29/2010 12:00:00 AM
Subscription Name: neudesicdemo
Offer Name: Windows Azure Platform Development Accelerator Extended

Total Consumed*:   674.000000 Compute Hours
Amount included with your offer: 750 Compute Hours
Amount over (under) your monthly average: -76.000000 Compute Hours

THE WINDOWS AZURE PRICING MODEL

Each service in the Windows Azure platform has its own metering model, and some services will charge you based on more than one factor. In addition, you are subject to bandwidth charges for nearly all platform services you make use of.

The pricing model is summarized below and its components are described in the sections that follow. Pricing models and rates could change over time, so it's important to verify the pricing information in this book is still current. To view the pricing model and rates for each service, visit Azure.com and navigate to the Pricing area, or go directly to http://www.microsoft.com/windowsazure/pricing/.

Consumption-based monthly pricing is the most popular way to use cloud computing but there are other options that can win you discounts. If you decide you are going to use the Windows Azure platform for some period of time, you can purchase a subscription offer for a term of 6 months or more and receive discounted pricing. In addition, if your organization negotiates software licensing with Microsoft through an Enterprise Agreement be aware that you can also negotiate Windows Azure pricing through that channel.

Many of the Windows Azure services charge by the gigabyte of consumption. A gigabyte (GB) is 2^{30} (1,073,741,824) bytes.

Windows Azure Platform Pricing Model (as of February 2011)

Service	Metering	Rate
Windows Azure Compute	VM instance	XS: $0.05 / hour / instance S: $0.12 / hour / instance M: $0.24 / hour / instance L: $0.48 / hour / instance XL: $0.96 / hour / instance
Windows Azure Storage	Storage size Transactions	$0.15 / GB / month $0.01 per 10,000 transactions
Content Delivery Network	Bandwidth Transactions	$0.15 / GB / month $0.01 per 10,000 transactions
Windows Azure Connect	To be announced	Currently in CTP
SQL Azure Database	Database size	$9.99 / GB / month (1-50GB)
SQL Azure Reporting	To be announced	Currently in CTP
SQL Azure Sync Service	To be announced	Currently in CTP
AppFabric Access Control	Transactions	$1.99 per 100,000 transactions
AppFabric Cache	To be announced	Currently in CTP
AppFabric Service Bus	Connections	$3.99 / connection (or buy packs)
DataMarket	Varies with data	See datamarket.azure.com
Most Services	Data transfers (bandwidth)	$0.10 / GB in, $0.15 out (NA, Europe) $0.10 / GB in, $0.20 out (Asia)

* Pricing as of February 2011. Be sure to confirm the latest rates at Azure.com.

Bandwidth Charges (Most Services)

There is one aspect of pricing that applies across the board to nearly every service and that is bandwidth (also called data transfers). Bandwidth charges apply whenever your use of a cloud service requires data transfers in or out of the data center. In North America and Europe, bandwidth costs you $0.10 / GB for data transfers into the data center and $0.15 / GB for transfers out. Bandwidth rates are higher in Asia: $0.10 / GB in, $0.20 / GB out.

Locale	Storage Charge Type	Cost / Month
N. America, Europe	Data Transfers in	$0.10 / GB / mo
N. America, Europe	Data Transfer out	$0.15 / GB / mo
Asia	Data Transfers in	$0.10 / GB / mo
Asia	Data Transfer out	$0.20 / GB / mo

Let's consider some examples. If you host a web application in the cloud and users access it in their browser, you're incurring bandwidth charges with each request and response. If you host a web service in the cloud and remote client programs access it, you're again incurring bandwidth charges. If your cloud application sends an email or invokes an external web service, you're incurring bandwidth charges. If you have a program in the enterprise that consumes a cloud database, you're incurring bandwidth charges.

Before you get too worried about this, remember you're only paying for bandwidth when you cross in and out of the data center. An example where you don't pay any bandwidth charges is when your hosted web application calls your hosted web service: if both are in the same data center, no bandwidth charges apply to that "internal" communication.

Windows Azure Compute Service

In the Windows Azure Compute service you are charged for virtual machine instances you reserve by the hour (active or not); and also for bandwidth. VMs come in multiple sizes each with its own hourly rate as shown below. The Extra Small instance is very limited and should be used cautiously. The Small size is the one most popularly used: a large number of applications can run comfortably on this size machine. Notice that as you progress from the Small to the Extra Large sizes, the number of cores, amount of RAM, network throughput, amount of local storage, and hourly rate double from the previous size.

Windows Azure Compute VM Sizes and Rates

Charge Type	VM Size	CPU Cores	RAM	Peak MBPS	Local Storage	Cost per Hour
Compute	Extra Small	Shared	768 MB	5	20 GB	$ 0.05
Compute	Small	1	1.7 GB	100	250 GB	$ 0.12
Compute	Medium	2	3.5 GB	200	500 GB	$ 0.24
Compute	Large	3	7 GB	400	1,000 GB	$0.48
Compute	Extra Large	4	15 GB	800	2,000 GB	$ 0.96
Bandwidth						Standard rates

TIP: If you are taking advantage of promotional offers that give you a certain amount of free Windows Azure Compute hours, check the details to see which VM Sizes are eligible.

Once you allocate a virtual machine instance in the Compute Service, you are paying for it at its hourly rate until such time as you deallocate it; a partial hour is charged as a full hour. You are always being charged, 24 x 7, regardless of how busy or idle a VM is at any particular moment. This is true regardless of whether the VM instance is in the Production slot or the Staging slot. For example, let's say you allocate 2 VM instances at the Small size. After one month this will cost you $0.12 x 2 instances x 24 hours x 30+ days, or about $175.

Windows Azure Storage Service

Windows Azure Storage is charged at the same rates regardless of whether you are using blobs, queues, and/or tables. You are charged in several ways based on storage size, storage transactions, and bandwidth.

Storage size is charged at $0.15 / GB / month, based on the average daily amount of storage. If you stored 1GB of data all month, you would be charged $0.15 for storage size. If you stored 30GB of data for 1 day, you'd be charged the same amount.

Since you are charged for the amount of data you store each month, it behooves you to consider lifetime policies for your data. Anything you leave in the cloud that doesn't need to be there is costing you money, month after month.

In addition to storage size, you are also charged for storage transactions such as storing data, retrieving data, and polling for data. Transactions cost $0.01 per 10,000 transactions. It's important to note the implications of this: some code that is innocent in the enterprise can be costly in the cloud, such as unnecessarily repetitive data access or tight polling loops.

A third way in which you'll be charged for storage is bandwidth. Storage access from outside the data center will subject you to bandwidth charges.

Charge Type	Cost / Month
Storage data size	$0.15 / GB / month
Transactions	$0.01 / 10,000 transactions
Bandwidth	Standard rates

One other way in which you might be charged for storage is if you make use of another service, the Content Delivery Network (CDN), which serves up blob storage through a worldwide network of edge servers for high performance.

Let's illustrate how these charges combine. If you store a 1MB image in blob storage and your cloud-hosted web site references it in a web page (i.e. in an HTML <IMG> tag), you will be paying first of all for the storage of that image file which will cost you $0.00015 a month. In addition, each time a user accesses a page on your web site that references the image, the browser will go out and fetch the image—incurring charges for the transaction ($0.000001) and bandwidth ($0.00015).

Windows Azure CDN Service

When the Content Delivery Network service is enabled for a storage account, charges are metered very similarly to Windows Azure Storage charges. Data transfers from the CDN edge servers cost $0.15 / GB in North America and Europe, and $0.20 / GB from other locations. In addition, as the CDN accesses your blob storage you are charged for storage transactions and bandwidth. Using the CDN adds additional costs to what you are already paying for storage but in return for using it you get high performance delivery worldwide.

Charge Type	Location	Cost / Month
CDN Data Transfer	N.A., Europe	$0.15 / GB / mo for transfers
CDN Data Transfer	Other locations	$0.20 / GB / mo for transfers
Transactions	All	$0.01 / 10,000 transactions
Storage Access	All	Standard rates
Bandwidth	All	Standard rates

SQL Azure Database Service

The SQL Azure Database service charges a flat monthly fee for each database based on a size bucket. Bandwidth charges also apply.

Databases are available in discrete sizes ranging from 1GB to 50GB. The smaller sizes are sold in a Web Edition and the larger sizes in a Business Edition. There is no feature difference between the two editions as of this writing but that could change in the future.

The rate for SQL Azure is $9.99/GB/month for the specified allotted size, regardless of how much of the database is in use. Thus, an empty 1GB database costs the same as a full 1GB database.

Charge Type	Edition	Size	Cost / Month
Database	Web	up to 1GB	$9.99
Database	Web	up to 5GB	$49.95
Database	Business	up to 10GB	$99.99
Database	Business	up to 20GB	$199.98
Database	Business	up to 30GB	$299.97
Database	Business	up to 40GB	$399.96
Database	Business	up to 50GB	$499.95
Bandwidth			Standard rates

The monthly fee for a database is amortized over the month and charged on a daily basis; you only pay for databases on the days they exist, based on the peak actual size as measured each day.

There is no charge for the Master database which holds system information. You cannot add your own tables to the Master database.

TIP: A SQL Azure database can be queried to determine database and bandwidth charges.

AppFabric Access Control Service

The AppFabric Access Control service charges by transaction. Bandwidth charges also apply.

Charge Type	Cost / Month
100,000 transactions	$1.99
Bandwidth	Standard rates

The cost for an ACS transaction is $1.99 per 100,000 transactions. This is not rounded up: you are only charged for the actual number of transactions utilized in a billing period.

AppFabric Service Bus

The AppFabric Service Bus charges by connection. You can pay for individual connections but can save appreciably by purchasing connection packs which are sold in bundles of 5, 25, 100, or 500 connections.

Connections	Cost / Month
Individual	$3.99
5-connection pack	$9.95
25-connection pack	$49.75
100-connection pack	$199.00
500-connection pack	$995.00
Bandwidth	Standard rates

Individual connections cost $3.99 per connection. You are charged based on the number of connections made each day.

Connection packs are charged daily pro-rata by dividing the number of connections by the number of days in the month. Note that you may only revise your connection pack configuration once per 7 days. If you exceed the number of connections in your connection pack subscription, the extra connections are charged at the individual connection rate.

DataMarket

The DataMarket service provides reference data by subscription. Each dataset has unique pricing, and some are free. Available data subscriptions and pricing can be viewed at http://datamarket.azure.com.

Other Services

The following services are in Community Technology Preview at the time of this writing and pricing has not yet been announced. Visit Azure.com to check availability and pricing.

- AppFabric Cache service
- SQL Azure Data Sync service
- SQL Azure OData service
- SQL Azure Reporting service
- Windows Azure Connect service

"HIDDEN COSTS" IN THE CLOUD

Cloud computing has real business benefits that can help the bottom line of most organizations. However, you may have heard about (or directly experienced) cases of sticker shock where actual costs were higher than expectations. These episodes are usually ascribed to "hidden costs" in the cloud which are sometimes viewed as gremlins you can neither see nor control. Some people are spooked enough by the prospect of hidden costs to question the entire premise of cloud computing. Is using the cloud like using a slot machine, where you don't know what will come up and you're usually on the losing end?

These costs aren't really hidden, of course: it's more that they're overlooked, misunderstood, or underestimated. Below we identify sources of these so-called "hidden costs" and shed light on them so that they're neither hidden nor something you have to fear.

1. Dimensions of Pricing

In my opinion the #1 contributor to unexpected billing is simply the number of dimensions there are to the pricing model. In effect, everything in the cloud is cheap but every kind of service represents an additional level of charge. To make it worse, as new features and services are added to the platform the number of billing considerations continues to increase.

As an example, let's consider that you are storing some images for your web site in Windows Azure blob storage and are using a data center in the United States. What does this cost you? The answer is, it doesn't cost you very much—but you might be charged in as many as 4 ways:

- Storage fees: Storage used is charged at $0.15/GB per month
- Transaction fees: Accessing storage costs $0.01 per 10,000 transactions

- Bandwidth fees: Sending or receive data in and out of the data center costs $0.10/GB in, $0.15/GB out
- Content Delivery Network: If you are using this optional edge caching service, you are also paying an additional $0.15/GB and an additional $0.01 per 10,000 transactions

You might still conclude these costs are reasonable after taking everything into account, but this example should serve to illustrate how easily you can inadvertently leave something out in your estimating. There is a positive aspect to this, which is that your billing is very transparent: the itemization lets you know exactly what you are being charged for.

What to do about it: You can guard against leaving something out in your calculations by using tools and resources that account for all the dimensions of pricing, such as:

- Microsoft's *Windows Azure TCO Calculator*
  http://www.microsoft.com/windowsazure/offers
- Neudesic's *Azure ROI Calculator*
  http://azureroi.cloudapp.net/
- The official Windows Azure pricing information
  http://www.microsoft.com/windowsazure/offers

With a thorough checklist in front of you, you won't fail to consider all of the billing categories. Also make sure that anything you look at is current and up to date as pricing formulas and rates can change over time. You also need to be as accurate as you can in predicting your usage in each of these categories.

2. Bandwidth

In addition to hosting and storage costs, your web applications are also subject to bandwidth charges (also called data transfer charges). When someone accesses your cloud-hosted web site in a web browser, the requests and responses incur data transfer charges. When an external client accesses your cloud-hosted web service, the requests and responses incur data transfer charges.

Bandwidth is often overlooked or underappreciated in estimating cloud computing charges. There are several reasons for this. First, it's not something we're used to having to measure. Second, it's less tangible than other measurements that tend to get our attention, such as number of servers and amount of storage. Third, it's usually down near the bottom of the pricing list so not everyone may notice it or pay attention to it. Lastly, it's nebulous: many have no idea what their bandwidth use is or how they would estimate it.

What to do about it: You can model and estimate your bandwidth using tools like Fiddler, and once running in the cloud you can measure actual bandwidth using mechanisms such as IIS logs. With a proper analysis of bandwidth size and breakdown, you can optimize your application to reduce bandwidth.

You can also exercise control over bandwidth charges through your solution architecture: you aren't charged for bandwidth when it doesn't cross in or out of the data center. For example, a web application in the cloud calling a web service in the same data center doesn't incur bandwidth charges.

3. Leaving the Faucet Running

As a father I'm constantly reminding my children to turn off the lights and not leave the faucets running: it costs money! Leaving an application deployed that you forgot about is a surefire way to get a surprising bill. Once you put applications or data into the cloud, they continue to cost you money, month after month, until such time as you remove them. It's very easy to put something in the cloud and forget about it.

What to do about it: Be proactive in recognizing the faucet has been left running before the problem reaches flood levels. First and foremost, review your bill regularly. You don't have to wait until end of month and be surprised: your Windows Azure bill can be viewed online anytime to see how your charges for the month are accruing. Second, make it someone's job to regularly review that what's in the cloud still needs to be there and that costs are in line with expectations. Set expiration dates or renewal review dates for your cloud applications and data. Third, consider where you can design automatic shutdown of compute instances and data into your solutions.

4. Compute Charges are not Based on Usage

If you put an application in the cloud and no one uses it, does it cost you money? Well, if a tree falls in the forest and no one is around to hear, does it make a noise? The answer to both questions is yes. Since the general message of cloud computing is consumption-based pricing, some people assume their hourly compute charges are based on how much their application is used. It's not the case: hourly charges for compute time do not work that way in Windows Azure. Rather, you are reserving machines and your charges are based on wall clock time per core. Whether those servers are very busy, lightly used, or not used at all doesn't affect this aspect of your bill. Where consumption-based pricing does enter the picture is in the number of servers you need to support your users, which you can increase or decrease at will. There are other aspects of your bill that are charged based on direct consumption such as bandwidth.

What to do about it: Understand what your usage-based and non-usage-based charges will be, and estimate costs accurately. Don't make the mistake of thinking an unused application left in the cloud is free—it isn't.

5. Staging Costs the Same as Production

If you deploy an application to Windows Azure, it can go in one of two places: your project's Production slot or its Staging slot. Many have mistakenly concluded that only Production is billed for when in fact Production and Staging are both charged for, and at the same rates.

What to do about it: Use Staging as a temporary area and set policies that anything deployed there must be deployed to Production or shut down within a certain amount of time. Give someone the job of checking for forgotten Staging deployments and deleting them—or even better, automate this process.

6. A Suspended Application is Still Billable

Applications deployed to Windows Azure Production or Staging can be in a *running* state or a *suspended* state. Only in the running state will an application be active and respond to traffic. Does this mean a suspended application does not accrue charges? Not at all—the wall clock-based billing charges accrue in exactly the same way regardless of whether your application is suspended or not.

What to do about it: Only suspend an application if you have good reason to do so, and this should always be followed by a more definitive action such as deleting the deployment or upgrading it and starting it up. It doesn't make any sense to suspend a deployment and leave it in the cloud: no one can use it and you're still being charged for it.

7. Seeing Double

Your cloud application will have one more software tiers, which means it is going to need one or more server farms. How many servers will you have in each farm? You might think a good answer is 1, at least when you're first starting out. In fact, you need a minimum of 2 servers per farm if you want the Windows Azure SLA to be upheld, which gives you 3½ 9's of availability (99.95%). If you're not aware of this, your estimates of compute hosting costs could be off by 100%!

The reason for this 2-server minimum is how patches and upgrades are applied to cloud-hosted applications in Windows Azure. The Fabric that controls the data center has an upgrade domain system where updates to servers are sequenced to protect the availability of your application. It's a wonderful system, but it doesn't do you any good if you only have 1 server.

What to do about it: If you need the SLA, be sure to plan on at least 2 servers per farm. If you can live without the SLA, it's fine to run a single server assuming it can handle your user load.

8. Polling

Polling data in the cloud is a costly activity. If you poll a queue in the enterprise and the queue is empty, this does not explicitly cost you money. In the cloud it does, because simply attempting to access storage (even if the storage is empty) is a transaction that costs you something. While an individual poll doesn't cost you much—only $0.01 per 10,000 transactions—it will add up to big numbers if you're doing it repeatedly.

What to do about it: Either find an alternative to polling, or do your polling in a way that is cost-efficient. There is an efficient way to implement polling using an algorithm that varies the sleep time between polls based on whether any data has been seen recently. When a queue is seen to be empty the sleep time increases; when a message is found in the queue, the sleep time is reduced so that message(s) in the queue can be quickly serviced.

9. Unwanted Traffic and DoS Attacks

If your application is hosted in the cloud, you may find it is being accessed by more than your intended user base. That can include curious or accidental web users, search engine spiders, and openly hostile denial of service (DoS) attacks by hackers or competitors. What happens to your bandwidth charges if your web site or storage assets are being constantly accessed by a bot?

Windows Azure does have some hardening to guard against DoS attacks but you cannot completely count on this to ward off all attacks, especially those of a new nature. Windows Azure's automatic applying of security patches will help protect you. If you enable the feature to allow Windows Azure to upgrade your Guest OS VM image, you'll gain further protections over time automatically. The firewall in SQL Azure Database will help protect your data. Unless you're willing to put up with the occasional downtime, you'll want to run at least 2 servers per farm so that rapidly-issued security patching does not disrupt your application's availability.

What to do about it: To defend against such attacks, first put the same defenses in place that you would for a web site in your perimeter network, including reliable security, use of mechanisms to defeat automation like CAPTCHA, and coding defensively against abuses such as cross-site scripting attacks. Second, learn what defenses are already built into the Windows Azure platform that you can count on. Third, perform a threat-modeling exercise to identify the possible attack vectors for your solution—then plan and build defenses. Diligent review of your accruing charges will alert you early on should you find yourself under attack and you can alert Microsoft.

10. New Management Responsibilities

Cloud computing reduces management requirements and labor costs because data centers handle so much for you automatically including provisioning servers and applying patches. It's also true—but often overlooked—that the cloud thrusts some <u>new</u> management responsibilities upon you. Responsibilities you dare not ignore at the risk of billing surprises.

What are these responsibilities? Regularly monitor the health of your applications. Regularly monitor your billing. Regularly review whether what's in the cloud still needs to be in the cloud. Regularly monitor the amount of load on your applications. Adjust the size of your deployments to match load.

The cloud's marvelous IT cost efficiency is based on adjusting deployments larger or smaller to fit demand. This only works if you regularly perform monitoring and adjustment. Failure to do so can undermine the value you're supposed to be getting.

What to do about it: Treat your cloud application and cloud data like any resource in need of regular, ongoing management. Monitor the state of your cloud applications as you would anything in your own data center. Review your billing charges regularly as you would any operational expense. Measure the load on your applications and adjust the size of your cloud deployments to match. Some of this monitoring and adjustment can be automated using the Windows Azure Diagnostic and Service Management APIs. Regardless of how much of it is done by programs or people, it needs to be done.

MANAGING COSTS EFFECTIVELY

If the dynamics of costs are so different in the cloud from the enterprise, how can you manage them effectively?

1. Team up with experts. Work with a consultant or Microsoft partner who is experienced in giving cloud assessments, delivering cloud migrations, and supporting and managing cloud applications operationally. You'll get the benefits of sound architecture, best practices, and prior experience. Learn from the successes and failures of others.

2. Go through the assessment process. A cloud computing assessment will help you scope cloud charges and migration costs correctly. It will also get you started on formulating cloud computing strategy and policies that will guard against putting applications in the cloud that don't make sense there.

3. Take advantage of automation. Buy or build cloud governance software to monitor health, activity, and cost. Have your monitoring infrastructure notify your operations personnel about changes in activity levels and the need to adjust deployment size; or even take action automatically.

4. Get your IT group involved in cloud management. IT departments are sometimes concerned that cloud computing will mean they will have fewer responsibilities and will be needed less. Here's an opportunity to give IT new responsibilities to manage and safeguard your company's use of cloud computing.

5. Architect for cost. Solutions designed for the cloud should take the cost dynamics into account. Cost should be a first-class consideration when weighing design alternatives.

6. Monitor your monthly bill and identify surprising trends early on, before they become expensive.

7. Give yourself permission to experiment. Realistically you should expect that getting good at predicting costs and managing billing will require some experimentation and experience.

BILLING EXAMPLES

Below are some examples of different uses of the Windows Azure platform and costs incurred. There is also a "What will it cost?" example from Microsoft you can view online at http://msdn.microsoft.com/en-us/library/ff803375.aspx.

Example 1: Small Business Web Site

A small business uses Windows Azure for their web site which customers use to place orders. They make use of the Windows Azure Compute service to host their web site and the SQL Azure Database to host their database. Over a month, their usage is as follows:

Service	Daily Usage	Monthly Usage	Monthly Cost
Windows Azure Compute	2 Small-size VMs, runs 24 hours / day	2 x 24 x 30 (1440) hours @ $0.12 / hour	$175
SQL Azure Database	250MB	250MB [1GB size] @ $9.99 / month	$9.99
Bandwidth	100 web users per day 60,000 bytes in per user 1,500,000 bytes out per user	3,000 users per month 180,000,000 bytes in (0.16GB) 4,500,000,000 bytes out (4.19GB)	$0.02 + $0.63 ($0.65)
Total			$186

Example 2: Corporate Departmental Solution

A department of a medium-size corporation runs an application in Windows Azure that includes a web site, web services, and background processes, all hosted in Windows Azure Compute. They make use of multiple SQL Azure databases as well as Windows Azure Storage for an archive of images. Over a month, their usage is as follows:

Service	Daily Usage	Monthly Usage	Monthly Cost
Windows Azure Compute	4 Small-size VMs (2 roles), runs 24 hours / day	4 x 24 x 30 (2880) hours @ $0.12 / hour	$351
Windows Azure Storage	100GB, 20,000 transactions	100GB, 600,000 transactions	$15 + $0.60 ($15.60)
SQL Azure Database	20GB	20GB [2 x 10GB size] @ $99.99 / month	$200
Bandwidth	1,000 web users per day 120,000 bytes in per user 3,000,000 bytes out per user	30,000 users per month 3,600,000,000 bytes in (3.5GB) 90,000,000,000 bytes out (83.8GB)	$0.34 + $12.57 ($12.91)
Total			$580

Example 3: Large Supply Chain Solution

A large enterprise runs a supply chain management solution in Windows Azure that is integrated with a large array of suppliers and is in constant communication about activity and forecasts. Many Windows Azure platform services are used. Over a month, their usage is as follows:

Service	Monthly Usage	Monthly Cost
Windows Azure Compute	20 Large-size VMs, 20 x 24 x 30 (14,400) hours @ $0.48 / hour, runs 24 x 7	$7,013
Windows Azure Storage	90,000GB storage size @ $0.15 / GB 15,000,000 transactions @ $0.01 / 10,000 tx	$1,350 + $15 ($1,365)
CDN	4,000GB data transfers @ $0.15 / GB	$600
SQL Azure Database	50 x 50GB @ $495.95 / month 100 x 1GB @9.99 / month	$24,800 + $999 ($25,799)
AppFabric Access Control	1,000,000 transactions @$1.99 / 100,000	$19.90
AppFabric Service Bus	500 connections / day @$995 / 500	$995
Bandwidth	25,000 GB in @ $0.10 / GB 45,000 GB out @ $0.15 / GB	$2,500 + $6,750 ($9,250)
Total		$45,042

CHAPTER SUMMARY

In this chapter we explored the Windows Azure pricing model and the mechanics of billing. We explained how to set up a billing account, purchase a subscription, and view and manage your bill using the Microsoft Online Customer Portal.

We explored the pricing model for each released service of the platform. Each service has its own method of metering, and some have multiple meters. In addition, for nearly all services you are subject to bandwidth charges when you make data transfers in or out of the data center.

We also discussed "hidden costs" in the cloud, meaning factors that can affect your billing charges that you should be aware of to avoid surprises.

Lastly, we provided several billing examples showing small, medium, and large scenarios.

PART II
PLANNING FOR
WINDOWS AZURE

4

EVALUATING
CLOUD COMPUTING

"Adventure is just bad planning."
—*Roald Amundsen, Norwegian Explorer*

Planning for cloud computing is an absolute necessity. Not everything belongs in the cloud, and even those applications that are well-suited may require revision. There are financial and technical analyses that should be performed. In this chapter we'll explain how to evaluate cloud computing responsibly. We'll answer these questions:

- What is the ideal rhythm for evaluating and adopting cloud computing?
- What is the value and composition of a cloud computing assessment?
- What should an organization's maturity goals be for cloud computing?

CLOUD COMPUTING EVALUATION RHYTHM

Most people and organizations are still in the early stages of learning about cloud computing. How do you advance from that initial stage to having adopted cloud computing (and be glad that you did)? There's an ideal rhythm for evaluating and adopting cloud computing, shown below. There are 4 phases: Awareness, Assessment, Experiment, and Adoption.

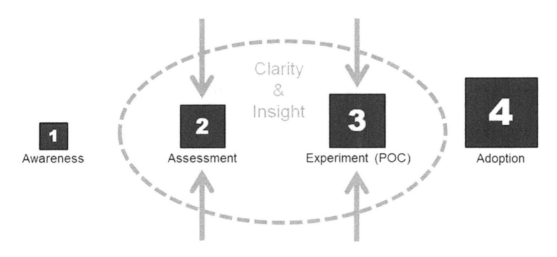

Ideal Rhythm for Evaluating Cloud Computing

Phases 2 and 3 are critical activities in moving from cloud spectator to cloud user. You need a plan for the cloud based on sound analysis, and an experiment in the cloud will give you a comfort level about the experience. Some organizations prefer to reverse the order of phases 2 and 3.

1. Awareness

In the *Awareness* phase, you're starting to learn about cloud computing and are forming an initial impression of it. You're likely getting information from many sources which might include the media, discussions with peers and colleagues, webcasts, conferences, vendor presentations, and the like. You're getting pummeled with information, partial information, and misinformation. There's a large buzz, but everything you're hearing is either generalized or is someone else's experience.

You're ready to move out of the awareness stage when you've heard enough general claims and want to know what cloud computing will mean *specifically* for your organization. That's what an assessment will give you.

2. Assessment

A cloud computing assessment has one purpose, and that is to bring the cloud into focus for your organization. A good cloud computing assessment will seek to answer these questions:

- Can I believe the claims of cloud computing?
- What is Microsoft doing in the cloud?
- What are the benefits?
- Is the cloud a good fit for my business?
- Where are the opportunities, and what ROI will they bring?
- How do I avoid risk?
- What does it cost?
- What belongs in the cloud and what doesn't?
- When is the right time to engage?

An assessment is very much like having a suit tailored to fit you perfectly. We move from the general to the specific. You'll exit the assessment with a clear understanding of how the cloud can benefit your company; a strategy that fits your business plans; a roadmap of opportunities; and a full view of risk/reward considerations. The roadmap your assessment produces will typically recommend a proof-of-concept and provide a prioritized timetable for cloud adoption. Some opportunities may make sense immediately but others may be more appropriate further out.

In determining the best timing for cloud projects, you should take into consideration your priorities, any significant business and IT events on the calendar, and the roadmap of upcoming Windows Azure features.

Armed with the clarity and plan that comes out of an assessment, you are ready for the next phase, an experiment.

3. Experiment

Although an assessment plays an important role in planning for the cloud, there's no substitute for some actual experience. A proof-of-concept experiment is recommended before you start adopting the cloud for production purposes. The experiment serves several purposes. First, it gives you an opportunity to test the claims of the cloud personally. In addition, the experience will either confirm the results of your assessment or cause you to revise your conclusions and plan.

Once you've concluded both an assessment and an experiment, you can proceed to cloud adoption with confidence.

4. Adoption

The final phase is actual adoption of the cloud. Your earlier assessment should have produced a roadmap for adoption, where some opportunities make sense in a "do them now" first wave and others in a potential second wave. After each migration to the cloud or new project in the cloud, you should reflect on the most recent experience and refine your cloud plans if warranted.

It's important to set up monitoring and management of your production applications in the cloud. If you expect fluctuating load you'll want to put a process in place to recognize when your deployment size needs to be adjusted.

CLOUD COMPUTING ASSESSMENTS

Typically a cloud computing assessment for Windows Azure will be performed by a Microsoft partner. Assessments are often made available for free so there's every reason to get one and use what comes out of it to guide your planning.

Whoever you bring in to perform a cloud computing assessment will likely have their own tools and process, but you should generally expect the activities listed below will be performed. If you'd like to see how we do cloud computing assessments at Neudesic visit http://cloud-assessment.com.

Envisioning

An envisioning session is an open and candid dialog between your business and technical decision makers about the cloud. The consultant leading the assessment will prompt roundtable discussions which will reveal areas of consensus and find the value propositions that align well with your business. Risks and concerns are also discussed. Doing this is important so you know where you stand at the start of the assessment; usually you will have a mixture of opinions about cloud computing in an organization. Knowing about interests and concerns will help guide what the assessment focuses on.

Chapter 5 describes how to perform envisioning.

Opportunity Discovery

Unless a company already knows which applications they want to put into the cloud, it's necessary to examine their portfolio of IT assets and identify potential candidates for the cloud. From the more promising candidates a short list of applications to analyze is produced. Even a large number of assets can be evaluated efficiently by identifying patterns and categories of applications and screening them against a playback of scenarios that are well-suited for the cloud. Both existing applications and new applications can be evaluated.

Chapter 6 describes how to hunt for cloud opportunities.

ROI Analysis

A Return on Investment (ROI) analysis examines whether moving an existing application to the cloud makes financial sense. For a new application you can still perform part of the calculation.

An ROI analysis begins by determining the Total Cost of Ownership (TCO) for the application on-premise, estimating what the TCO will be in the cloud, and comparing the two to determine savings. If the monthly cost of operation is less in the cloud, it's worth looking deeper. In order to figure out your overall savings, multiply your monthly savings times the expected lifetime of the application.

TCO and savings are only part of the picture. You also need to look at the cost of getting into the cloud. There's usually some level of development work involved in migrating an application to the cloud. Although migration is a one-time cost and savings are ongoing, it's still possible for migration costs to outweigh savings. Your ROI then is your anticipated overall savings minus your migration costs.

Chapter 9 describes how to calculate TCO and ROI.

Suitability Analysis

Determining the suitability of an application for the cloud clarifies whether it makes sense there. Suitability scoring also allows you to comparatively rank multiple applications in your IT portfolio to determine which among them are the leading candidates.

Scoring suitability requires considering and integrating multiple factors that range from technical compatibility to service level requirements to regulatory compliance.

Chapter 7 describes how to profile applications and score suitability.

Strategy

Formulating a strategy for your use of cloud computing is wise: it provides guidance people in your organization can use as a high level benchmark for whether a particular use of the cloud is appropriate. Your strategy should identify the leading reason(s) you will be using cloud computing, such as:

- Reducing cost
- Increasing corporate agility
- Adding additional capacity
- Disaster recovery
- Sustaining an experimental initiative
- Enabling a new business model
- Outsourcing aspects of IT

Your strategy should also define whether the cloud is in a minority or majority position: will new initiatives default to being on-premise or in the cloud?

Here's an example of a cloud computing strategy statement:

At Contoso, we have decided to leverage cloud computing to our advantage as the preferred way to host our public web properties. We will review suitability on a case-by-case basis, but the initial assumption is that public web-oriented applications will generally go into the cloud and internal applications will not. Our expectation is that we will save on IT costs and be able to respond quickly and effortlessly to changes in load which are often seasonal for our business. We have identified a task force to issue policies around use of cloud computing in the organization and act as a clearing house for approval.

You may not be able to define a strategy right away, and even once you have one expect to periodically revisit it and update it. Consider it a living document. Over time, you'll likely broaden your acceptable uses of cloud computing as your comfort level increases from positive experiences.

Chapter 10 describes adoption strategies for Windows Azure.

Roadmap

An assessment should produce a roadmap of cloud projects, prioritized and placed on a timeline.

Some cloud projects may make sense to pursue immediately. If there's significant savings to be gained by migrating a solution to the cloud, the sooner you migrate the sooner you start to reap the savings.

For other cloud projects it may make sense to wait. If a needed feature is coming to your cloud platform in 6 or 12 months, you should schedule your project to coincide with its availability. You might schedule a cloud project for the next fiscal year if you can't afford the development expenses out of this year's budget.

Your cloud projects should be sensibly scheduled to align with significant business and IT events on your calendar. Business events such as new products, services, and locations might influence the timing of your cloud projects. IT events such as server refresh cycles, data center planning, and roll-out of new systems should also be taken into account.

ORGANIZATIONAL MATURITY

Like most technical disciplines, your organization will need time and experience to become adept at cloud computing. Understanding the levels of maturity an organization can reach will help you guide your activities to promote increasing maturity. While there's no formal maturity model for Windows Azure yet, we can talk broadly about basic vs. advanced capabilities an organization should pursue.

Dept. / Group	Skill	Basic	Advanced
Analysts	Cost prediction	Predict costs correctly within an order of magnitude	Predict costs expertly Sophistication in cutting costs through creative applications of Windows Azure Windows Azure is a source of revenue for the organization (for example via DataMarket)
Decision Makers	Strategy	Experiment with Windows Azure to determine business value	Windows Azure is core to the organization's business strategy
Architects & Developers	Migration & Design	Experiment with Windows Azure to gain technical experience	Existing applications can be reliably migrated to Windows Azure New applications are designed for Windows Azure
IT workers	Management	Windows Azure solutions are deployed and managed	Windows Azure is expertly managed Deployments are instrumented for monitoring, autoscale, and disaster recovery Windows Azure is a central part of IT culture Windows Azure is integrated into governance and risk management processes

At its zenith, organizational maturity in cloud computing means it becomes central to how you do things: part of your business strategy, an inherent consideration in technical design, and core to your IT culture. This is discussed at length in Chapter 10, *Adoption Strategies*.

CHAPTER SUMMARY

In this chapter we described how to explore, evaluate, experiment with, and adopt Windows Azure. We recommended a 4-step rhythm of Awareness, Assessment, Experimentation, and Adoption. In the Awareness phase you are learning about cloud computing generally. In the Assessment phase you are analyzing what the cloud would mean specifically for your company and creating a plan. In the Experimentation phase you are trying a proof-of-concept project to get direct experience with the platform and validate its claims. In the Adoption phase you are using the platform in production.

We reviewed an assessment process that openly discusses risk vs. reward, discovers potential opportunities, and vets them through sound financial and technical analysis. The activities in the assessment process are detailed in the chapters that follow: envisioning risk and reward (Chapter 5), identifying opportunities (Chapter 6), profiling applications (Chapter 7), estimating migration (Chapter 8), calculating TCO and ROI (Chapter 9), and adoption strategies (Chapter 10).

5

ENVISIONING RISK & REWARD

"You can measure opportunity with the same yardstick that measures the risk involved. They go together."
—*Earl Nightingale*

"Take calculated risks. That is quite different from being rash."
—*George Patton*

In order to make an informed decision about Windows Azure you need more than a mere understanding of what cloud computing is; you also need to determine what it will mean for your company. In this chapter we'll answer these questions:

- How do you find the cloud computing synergies for your organization?
- How do you air and address risks and concerns about cloud computing?
- How will cloud computing affect your IT culture?

ENVISIONING

An envisioning session is a dialog between your business and technical decision makers about the cloud. The consultant leading the assessment will share insights and prompt discussions but the primary intent is to have your people share their thoughts, interests, and concerns about cloud computing with each other. Typically you will find a mixture of opinions about cloud computing in an organization. Knowing everyone's interests and concerns will allow the assessment activities to focus on what matters. Envisioning is part dreaming and part reality check!

Activities

An envisioning session is only the most visible activity in what is really an ongoing conversation within a company. Prior to this event some useful preparatory activities are an educational presentation and advance information gathering through interviews or surveys. During a formal assessment, roundtable discussions bring your business and technical decision makers together for an open and candid conversation about where cloud computing can take your company. This will usually reveal areas of consensus and help identify the potential areas of opportunity for cloud computing. Follow-up activities include profiling and analyzing candidate uses for cloud; formulating a cloud computing strategy; and creating an adoption plan and timetable.

Individual Perceptions: Interviews & Surveys

It's useful to ask up front what your perceptions of cloud computing are and hear from each stakeholder individually. You'll find some people already have a positive or negative view of the cloud while others haven't learned enough yet to form an opinion about it. It's best to do this early on before anyone has been swayed by the strongly-held opinions of others: you'll find out the most and there will be more ideas to discuss. One way to find out where individuals stand on cloud computing ahead of time is to send out surveys in advance of the envisioning session. In order for these to be useful you need to collect them in time to share the results at the envisioning session. A sample survey follows.

Education: Presentations & Demos

Often a company will have learned some things about cloud computing prior to starting a cloud computing assessment but their understanding may be partial or even incorrect. Providing a presentation or demonstration such as a "lunch and learn" in advance is often a good idea to share specific information about the Windows Azure platform to business or technical audiences.

For education on the Windows Azure platform, key points to review are:

- Cloud computing basics
- What Microsoft is doing in cloud computing
- Capabilities of the Windows Azure Platform
- Business benefits
- Technical benefits
- Overview of functional areas – Windows Azure, SQL Azure, AppFabric
- Success stories
- An assessment as the next step in evaluating Windows Azure

On the day of the envisioning session, it's also wise to include a short educational review of capabilities and benefits: it ensures all attendees have the same basic information about cloud computing fresh in their minds.

Microsoft Cloud Computing Assessment – Stakeholder Survey

Instructions: Please provide any of the information below that you are comfortable sharing about your opinions of cloud computing. Please mail back to <name@company.com>

1. Prior Experience. Do you have any prior experience with cloud computing? How did it go?

2. Intended Use. Do you have a potential use for cloud computing in mind?

3. Questions. What questions do you have about cloud computing?

4. Proof. What demonstration or experiment would help you make a cloud computing decision?

5. Benefits. What benefits do you expect cloud computing might bring your organization? (check all that apply)

- ❑ Reduce Costs / Control Costs
- ❑ Convert CapEx to OpEx / Eliminate up-front hardware purchases
- ❑ Increased Flexibility / Elasticity
- ❑ Agility / Faster Time to Market
- ❑ Greater Capacity / Scale
- ❑ Free up Data Center / Extend Data Center
- ❑ Increased Accessibility / Globalization
- ❑ Automated Management / Simplify IT
- ❑ Innovation / Competitive Edge
- ❑ Leverage the SaaS Model for your application
- ❑ Curious about Cloud / Cloud Experiment
- ❑ Other:

6. Concerns. Do you have concerns/doubts about cloud computing? (check all that apply)

- ❑ Security
- ❑ Performance
- ❑ Service Level Agreement concerns
- ❑ Technology is not ready
- ❑ Does not align well with technologies we use
- ❑ Data sensitivity / vulnerability
- ❑ Regulatory compliance
- ❑ Cost
- ❑ Vendor lock-in
- ❑ Lack of in-house expertise
- ❑ Skeptical of value
- ❑ Other:

Thank you!

Reward Discussion

Cloud computing offers many different areas of benefit but they will not be of equal appeal to any one company. Cost reduction isn't the only justification for cloud computing. It's necessary to acquaint your decision makers with the broad benefits story in order to find out what resonates.

The Windows Azure value proposition is discussed later in this chapter in the section, *Discovering the Values that Resonate*.

Risk Discussion

Any benefits discussion needs to be balanced with a discussion of risks, concerns, and security. Whether real or perceived, concerns need to be aired, treated seriously, and mitigated to the satisfaction of the stakeholders.

Commonly cited concerns are discussed later in this chapter in the section, *Confronting Risks and Concerns*.

Opportunity Capture

An important outcome of the envisioning process is to have identified potential cloud computing opportunities worthy of further study. Be sure to capture a list of potential opportunities to analyze from the discussion. Throughout the envisioning session keep an ear out for attendees who express interest in the cloud: this usually means they have one or more opportunities in mind.

Your company may already have a strong opportunity in mind for the cloud prior to the assessment; even so, the envisioning process serves as a proving ground for ensuring you have considered all the possibilities and discussed risk and reward openly.

If you can't come up with at least one cloud computing opportunity from envisioning then the other assessment activities won't be needed. You may want to establish criteria for resurrecting the conversation at a future time.

Common patterns and anti-patterns that indicate fitness for the Windows Azure platform are discussed in Chapter 6, *Identifying Opportunities*.

IT Culture Discussion

Companies vary on their IT culture and how they approach risk vs. reward. Being aware of this will help in properly weighing pros vs. cons and determining the best timing for cloud computing.

Using Gartner's definitions, there are 3 basic categories. There's the Aggressive Innovator who values reward over risk and has gotten good at managing risk in order to get the brass ring; there's the Pragmatic Adopter who looks at risk and reward equally; and there's the Risk-Averse company who is hesitant to consider risks of any kind. If you're in the first two categories you're more likely to take an early look at cloud computing.

Strategy Discussion

It's wise to have a strategy for cloud computing. For some organizations, the right role for cloud computing is clear from the onset. For others experimentation and experience are necessary before a strategy can be realized. Expect that continued use of the Windows Azure platform will suggest more and more valuable uses. For more information on strategy, see Chapter 10, *Adoption Strategies*.

DISCOVERING THE VALUES THAT RESONATE

Cloud computing has multiple benefits. While this is good, there's the danger that some of your people may not be acquainted with all of the benefits and have a one-dimensional view of the cloud. In addition, getting specific about platform allows us to talk about benefits more concretely. We can only talk generally about the benefits of *cloud computing* but we can get very specific about the benefits of the *Windows Azure Platform*. Let's do so now.

Financial Benefits	• Reduced Cost
	• Consumption-based Pricing
	• Convert CapEx to OpEx
Scalability	• Capacity on Tap
	• Reliability
	• Service Level Agreement
Streamlining IT	• Simplify IT
	• Automated Management
	• Self-Service IT
Agility & Flexibility	• Faster Time to Market
	• Elasticity
	• No Commitment
Competitive Advantage	• Levels the Playing Field
	• New Capabilities
	• New Business Models

In an envisioning session, it's useful to gauge the level of interest in each of these areas one-by-one. You'll sometimes find strong consensus about certain areas of interest which tells you you've found an area of synergy that strongly resonates for the company.

Financial Benefits

Reduced Cost

Most organizations can reduce their IT costs by leveraging cloud computing. In my experience it's not unusual to see a 30-40% savings in monthly costs after moving to the cloud, in line with many analyst predictions, and I've seen cases where the reduction in costs has been as much as 90%. Everyone's mileage varies of course and you need to study your applications to determine what your level of savings will be. This is one reason why a cloud computing assessment is so essential: it attaches dollar signs to the opportunities.

If you've already invested in a data center, you could argue that moving only a few applications to the cloud doesn't amount to any real savings since you continue to operate that data center and still have your on-premise expenses. That could be so in the short term, but at some point moving to the cloud will make a financial difference. You'll likely be able to reduce the size of your data center, avoid expanding it, or curtail your spending on server upgrade cycles.

Consumption-based Pricing

Cloud computing's billing model is based on metered, consumption-based pricing. Only paying for what you use, only for as long as you need it, is highly cost-efficient. This model benefits you the most if you have fluctuation or uncertainty in demand and application lifetime.

Consumption-based pricing can be a double-edged sword, as anyone knows who has been surprised by a utility bill. Cloud computing does bring with it the need to regularly look at your monthly bills and manage your consumption. In Windows Azure you don't have to wait until the end of the month to find out how your billing is trending: you can look up your bill-to-date online anytime.

Convert CapEx to OpEx

Capital expenditures are converted to operational expenditures in the cloud. Those server purchases and (periodic server refresh cycles every few years) simply don't exist when you use cloud computing, replaced by your pay-as-you-go monthly bill. This makes it possible to have business initiatives that pay for their IT assets as they operate without the traditional barriers of getting budget and approval for up-front hardware spending (and the IT work that comes with it).

Scalability

Capacity on Tap

Historically, for enterprises to ensure they had adequate capacity they either had to build out sufficiently large infrastructure or make arrangements to have extra capacity on standby. Both options can be expensive and wasteful. If you build out your data center to support peak demand, you may have a lot of that computing power being unused during times of lesser demand. If you are paying to reserve a second data center but aren't using it all the time, you are again wasting money. Even these measures may not be sufficient if you haven't been able to accurately forecast what the future holds in terms of demand.

Windows Azure provides you with all the capacity on tap you could possibly need via some of the world's largest and finest data centers. You won't outgrow Windows Azure. Best of all, you *pay nothing* to reserve this capacity; you simply use it at the time you need it, and only for as long as you need it.

Reliability

Windows Azure provides you with a highly reliable environment. The availability of your applications and the integrity of your data are protected through redundancy and managed oversight. Many layers of physical and network protection guard your IT assets.

Service Level Agreement (SLA)

Windows Azure services come with a service level agreement. Each service has its own service level details which you can find on Azure.com but it boils down to 3 9's (99.9%) availability generally and 3½ 9's (99.95%) availability for compute hosting. That means you might experience 6-8 hours of unavailability during a calendar year. There's no way to predict if that will occur or when it might occur.

Your reaction to the Windows Azure SLA could be positive, neutral, or negative depending on your requirements and what you're getting right now on-premise or from your current hosting environment. There's no means available to you to improve on the SLA, so it either fits your needs or it doesn't. It should be noted that the Windows Azure SLA is a starting point: your application could degrade your service level if it has a poor design, poor implementation, or is poorly maintained.

You should also know that for hosting the Windows Azure SLA is only provided if you run at least 2 servers in a farm, something you need to factor into your estimation of costs. The reason for this is that availability during patching and software updates is maintained by sequencing server updates. When there's only one server, sequencing isn't possible and there will be occasional interruptions in availability.

Streamlining IT

Simplify IT

Windows Azure simplifies some aspects of IT, performing them automatically or at the click of a button. The following tasks are examples of activities that are easy to perform through the Windows Azure portal:

- Create (or delete) a hosted cloud service
- Create (or delete) a storage account
- Create (or delete) a relational database
- Deploy new or updated software
- Expand or reduce the size of a deployment
- Promote/Swap between Staging and Production
- Backup, restore, or synchronize data

The simplification of IT that Windows Azure offers may allow you to reallocate certain tasks to more junior people in your IT department, or may allow your IT department to be more responsive.

Automated Management

Windows Azure also provides automatic management for you. For example, patches are automatically applied to your servers. Application health is monitored. Defensive actions are taken in response to denial of service attacks.

Self-Service IT

I've never come across an IT department that wasn't busy, and the inevitable result is that work requiring the attention of IT professionals must be prioritized and bottlenecks form. I think IT is at its best when it finds ways to empower departments and individuals to do their own IT, safely and reliably. This brings up the issue of IT culture and how your company feels about "the democratization of IT".

Some companies are committed to this concept; some are open to it; and some are opposed to it.

Agility & Flexibility

Faster Time-to-Market

For many companies, the process of procuring hardware, configuring servers, and deploying applications can be extremely time-consuming, taking anywhere from 6 weeks to 6 months. Your delays may be aggravated further by process, the need to get budget approvals, and where you are prioritized vis-à-vis other projects.

Windows Azure can take you to a completely different place, the world of on-demand IT. How does 20 minutes sound in comparison? That's how long it takes to deploy your software to as many servers as you want in a Windows Azure data center. To think is to act.

Elasticity

Elasticity is the "rubber band" aspect of the cloud which allows you to expand or reduce your deployment whenever you choose. Elasticity is what gives the cloud its amazing cost-efficiency because you only pay for what you use and only use what you need.

In Windows Azure changing the size of a deployment is a simple operation you can initiate through a management portal. It takes about 20 minutes to spin up additional servers. Adding or removing server instances won't affect the availability of your application (keeping in mind you need at least 2 servers in a farm to qualify for the SLA). Automatic adjustment of your deployment is not a built-in feature of the platform today but it is possible for you to create your automation programmatically.

No Commitment

Unlike traditional hosting where you may be used to leasing a set amount of resource for a certain number of years, cloud computing doesn't require you to commit to a term or a certain level of usage. From your perspective, there's no commitment.

Windows Azure is an easy-in/easy-out environment. You can jump into the cloud whenever you want, stay as long as you want, and leave when you want. You can walk away cleanly, with no residual legal or financial obligations beyond your current month's bill.

By the way, you can play the commitment card both ways to your advantage. Paying monthly and without a commitment may give you comfort when you are first getting started with the cloud. Once you decide you are going to be using Windows Azure on a regular basis, Microsoft will offer you discounted rates if you're willing to make commitment. You can get term-based subscriptions. If your enterprise has an EA agreement with Microsoft you can also negotiate commitment and rate through that channel.

Competitive Advantage

Levels the Playing Field

Historically, only larger companies in more industrialized nations could afford first class data centers. Cloud computing levels the playing field, allowing smaller companies and individuals to compete on an equal footing from an IT standpoint—even in developing nations.

New Capabilities

Windows Azure brings offers new capabilities not previously available in the enterprise. One of these is a federated security service, allowing you to support a broad set of security schemes for use with external customers and partners. Another is a service bus, allowing you to communicate easily with other organizations across network boundaries and firewalls without requiring infrastructure changes from IT.

New Business Model

The Software-as-a-Service business model may be something you're interested in operating yourself. Cloud computing is the best way to offer SaaS, where you operate a single deployment of your solution in the cloud, supporting multiple tenants. Your operating costs are low and efficient, and you can easily adjust the deployment larger or smaller as your clientele demand changes.

CONFRONTING RISKS AND CONCERNS

Concerns are natural with any new wave technology—especially with something as big and paradigm-shifting as cloud computing. Whether real or perceived, concerns from stakeholders and their trusted people need to be acknowledged, treated respectfully, and addressed to their satisfaction. Concerns about the cloud generally fall into 3 categories: security, risks, and impact.

The issue at the heart of most cloud computing concerns is *trust*, pure and simple. Trust is something that can be earned, and earned incrementally. As you start to experiment with Windows Azure, your comfort level will increase and a certain level of trust will be established. As you use it more extensively, your trust level will increase.

Security

Security often comes up when companies are considering cloud computing. Security concerns can be grouped into 3 major categories:

- General, non-specific concerns about security
- Specific security concerns
- Regulatory requirements imposed by industry or government

A revealing exercise to perform when considering a cloud security concern is to invert the problem and ask, "How do you guard against that now?" It may be that the same defenses being used in the enterprise can be applied in the cloud.

General Security Concerns

People concerned about security in the cloud aren't always able to articulate specific issues. If you can't get specific, it's best to get acquainted with the security features of cloud data centers and then review some of the most commonly-raised security concerns and how they can be addressed.

The more you learn about Windows Azure data center security the more comfortable you will feel. Microsoft invests heavily in security and its data centers are extremely secure—very likely more secure than your data center. The security features of Windows Azure data centers are described in Chapter 2 under *Data Center Security*. For further detail see the Microsoft whitepaper *Windows Azure Security Overview*, available at http://go.microsoft.com/?linkid=9740388.

Specific Security Concerns

When security concerns are specific, they can be discussed, modeled, and defended against concretely. Most security concerns have of course been raised in the past by others and have known defenses. The commonly raised security concerns are described on the next page along with their mitigations. When a new security concern is raised, the right thing to do is model it, identifying the vectors of attack and planning defenses. Threat modeling is explained later in this chapter.

Notice that mitigations often require a partnership between Microsoft and the enterprise, each doing their part. You can and should add your own security layer alongside what the cloud gives you.

Also notice that encrypting data you store and transmit, while not a cure-all for every ill, is one of the most important single things you can do. For this to be effective, you need to use a strong encryption method and protect and rotate your keys

Security Concern	Mitigation (Microsoft)	Mitigation (Customer)
Data falling into the wrong hands.	Data center has multiple isolation mechanisms to protect tenant data.	Encrypt all data your application transmits and stores.
Data loss.	Data centers store data with triple redundancy.	Back up your data.
Denial of Service (DoS) attacks.	Data centers are hardened, have DoS detection mechanisms, and take remedial actions such as blocking suspicious activity.	Provide standard protections against DoS in your application such as use of CAPCHA logins.
Abuse by insider with privileged access to your IT assets.	Control and audit personnel access, privileges, and security procedures.	Control and audit personnel access, privileges, and security procedures.
Network intruder gaining access to your IT assets.	Elaborate firewalls and intrusion detection systems.	Encrypt all data your application transmits and stores.
Observation of your data in transit by a hacker.		Use secure communication.
Man-in-the-Middle (MITM) attacks.		Use secure communication and ensure your client code validates server certificates.
Personally Identifiable Information (PII) disclosed to unauthorized parties.		De-personalize the data. Encrypt all data your application transmits and stores.
Security vulnerabilities in software.	Security patches applied automatically to your server instances.	Threat model your application's vulnerabilities and design defenses.

Security Concerns and Mitigations

Regulatory Requirements

Some organizations are subject to government or industry regulations about their data center, data, or applications. Some examples:

- Some government agencies must keep their digital assets on-premise.
- Some countries have laws that data must remain in the owner's country.
- Some organizations require certifications to demonstrate compliance, such as PCI/DSS for payment systems or FISMA for government agencies.

Many of these regulations and certifications pre-date cloud computing and as such some of them need revision or even legislative action before cloud computing data centers can qualify.

Consider who the responsible party is for demonstrating compliance: it might be the data center, it might be the application/data owner, or it might encompass both. If you have a compliance requirement, analyze which of the following categories it falls into.

1. *Compliance is your responsibility.* If the nature of compliance has to do with application and data and not the data center—areas that are completely in your control—then being compliant is in your hands.
2. *Windows Azure is in already in compliance.* Some certifications such as SAS70 and FISMA have already been attained by Windows Azure data centers; if the certification you need is already achieved you can rest easy.
3. *Windows Azure lacks a needed certification.* If a needed certification is not present, it may not be the right time to move your application to Windows Azure. Sometimes you can work around this problem by dividing your application into 2 parts, one that needs certification and one that doesn't; the latter portion can still go into the cloud. For example, if you need PCI certification for the payment portion of your application but not the rest of it you

could put most of your application in the cloud and invoke an external facility to handle payments.

4. *Moving Off-Premise is Not Permitted*. This would seem to put cloud computing out of the running but there is a way to bring Windows Azure on premise: the *Windows Azure Appliance*. Not everyone will have the budget for this approach but for sufficiently large organizations it's a viable option to consider. As of this writing the Windows Azure Appliance has been announced but is not yet available for purchase.

Governance, Risk & Compliance (GRC)

The areas of governance, risk management, and compliance have long been important to corporate bodies but until recently they had been considered independently. It has been found this can undermine their effectiveness. "GRC" is the treatment of governance, risk management, and compliance as an integrated set of concerns, an approach that has been growing in popularity ever since the US Sarbanes-Oxley Act (SOX). Each of the 3 GRC disciplines consists of 4 components: strategy, processes, technology and people. To apply GRC (to cloud computing as well as your other IT environments), it needs become an organizational discipline.

To help organizations understand what cloud computing means for GRC, the Cloud Security Alliance has published a document, *Security Guidance for Critical Areas of Focus in Cloud Computing V2*, available online at http://www.cloudsecurityalliance.org/csaguide.pdf. The recommendations below are largely inspired by its recommendations. Since cloud computing is young, it's not practical to implement all of them today, at least not in their fullest sense. Attending to these matters is best considered an ongoing activity, where you can achieve deeper levels of GRC with cloud computing as the industry matures.

Governance Recommendations

- Invest a portion of the savings from cloud computing in increased security scrutiny, assessments and audits.

- Pursue the development of security governance, best viewed as a shared responsibility of providers and customers.

- Review security governance provisions, auditing, and available metrics when evaluating a cloud computing provider.

- Seek collaborative security processes between the cloud computing provider and your organization.

- Look for security guarantees to be incorporated into Service Level Agreements so that they are enforceable.

Risk Management Recommendations

- Recognize that SLAs and contracts play a greater role in risk management than within the enterprise because you don't have direct physical control over the infrastructure.

- Expect security audits and assessments to be different from in other environments due to the on-demand, multi-tenant nature of cloud computing.

- Study of risks should include not only the cloud computing provider organization but also the specific services to be consumed.

- Adopt a risk management framework and maturity model and apply them consistently to your on-premise assets and your cloud computing assets.

- Treat cloud computing risk analysis as a supply chain.

Compliance Recommendations

- Involve your legal, contracts, IT, and security personnel when contracting cloud computing services. Watch out for rogue departments or individuals skirting these controls unless they are merely experimenting with non-production assets.

- Ensure you have a means of requesting security audits.
- Analyze the current compliance regulations you are subject to in light of planned cloud computing uses to determine if revisions are necessary to the regulations or to the IT plans.

Become fully acquainted with the security mechanisms and compliance provisions the cloud computing provider offers, including any optional or on-demand activities.

IT Impact

It's not unusual for IT departments to have conflicted feelings about cloud computing, being simultaneously drawn to the benefits while feeling uneasy and unsure about what the impact will be. Concerns about the impact of cloud computing may be felt by individuals or an entire department. Some common concerns are discussed below.

Will cloud computing be dangerous to the organization?

Cloud computing won't be dangerous to your organization if you follow best practices and especially if IT is participating in the evaluation and adoption of cloud computing, providing guidance and support. It's when cloud computing happens spontaneously around you, uncontrolled and uncoordinated, that's someone might do something unwise such as unintentionally exposing sensitive data.

Will cloud computing create chaos?

Not if you get out in front of it. Cloud computing can be adopted in a measured, organized way if IT can provide the necessary leadership and guidance early on. Let's acknowledge however that cloud computing is a disruptive technology. It brings new opportunities and new ways of doing things but it can also shake up the status quo a bit.

Will cloud computing put us in the position of being held responsible for IT we have no control over?

You have as much control over your assets in the cloud as you would in traditional hosting.

Will cloud computing make our job harder?

Cloud computing should make your job easier, not harder. Like developers, IT workers will need to learn some new tricks (and forget some old ones). Once ramped up, you'll be glad for all the things cloud computing does for you.

Will cloud computing make IT less relevant?

Cloud computing can make the IT department <u>more</u> relevant if IT leads the way on the cloud, guides and supports its use, and manages cloud assets.

Will cloud computing take away jobs?

Cloud computing will likely <u>change</u> the jobs of IT workers but it would take a very deep adoption level before it might impact staffing levels. Although cloud computing does automate many management tasks it doesn't automate all of them; in addition, cloud computing adds some new management responsibilities.

Will cloud computing make our skills obsolete?

Cloud computing won't obsolete anyone's skills but it may change the tasks that are most in demand.

Threat Modeling

One highly useful technique for analyzing security issues and designing defenses is threat modeling, a security analysis technique long used at Microsoft. Threat modeling is useful in any software context including cloud computing. It's useful because technical and non-technical people alike can follow the diagrams easily.

BEST PRACTICE: Use threat modeling to analyze security concerns and design mitigations.

To illustrate how threat modeling works in a cloud computing context, let's address a specific threat. A common concern is that the use of shared resources in the cloud might compromise the security of your data by allowing it to fall into the wrong hands—what we'll call a *Data Isolation Failure*. A data isolation failure is one of the risks many organizations considering cloud computing worry about.

To create our threat model, we'll start with the end result we're trying to avoid: data in the wrong hands.

Threat 1
Data in the
wrong hands

Next we need to think about what can lead to this end result that we don't want. How could data of yours in the cloud end up in the wrong hands? It seems this could happen deliberately or by accident. We can draw two nodes, one for deliberate compromise and one for accidental compromise; we number the nodes so that we can reference them in discussions. Either one of these conditions is sufficient to cause data to be in the wrong hands, so this is an OR condition.

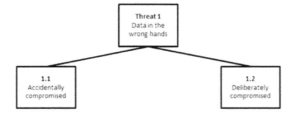

Let's identify the causes of *accidental data compromise* (1.1). One would be human failure to set the proper restrictions in the first place: for example, leaving a commonly used or easily-guessed database password in place. Another might be a failure on the part of the cloud infrastructure to enforce security properly. Yet another cause might be hardware failure, where a failed drive is taken out of the data center for repair. These and other causes are added to the tree, which now looks like this:

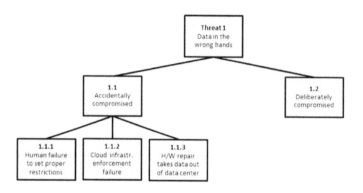

We can now do the same for the *deliberately compromised* branch (1.2). Some causes include an inside job, which could happen within your business but could also happen at the cloud provider. Another deliberate compromise would be a hacker observing data in transmission. These and other causes could be developed further, but we'll stop here for now.

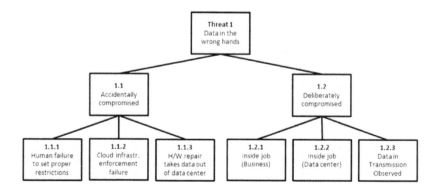

Once the tree is sufficiently developed, we can explore mitigations to the root causes, the bottom leaves of the tree. These mitigations are shown in circles in the diagram below (no mitigation is shown for the "data in transmission observed" node because it needs to be developed further). For cloud threat modeling I like to color code my mitigations to show the responsible party: green for the business, yellow for the cloud provider, red for a third party.

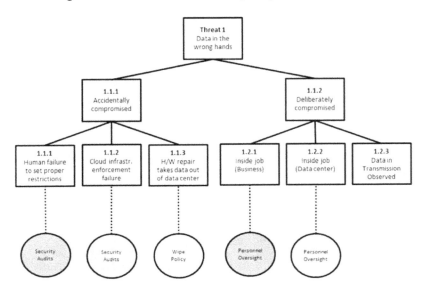

You should not start to identify mitigations until your threat tree is fully developed, or you'll go down rabbit trails thinking about mitigations rather than threats. Stay focused on the threats. I have deliberately violated this rule just now in order to show why it's important. At the start of this article we identified the threat we were trying to model as "data in the wrong hands". That was an insufficiently described threat, and we left out an important consideration: is the data intelligible to the party that obtains it? While we don't want data falling into the wrong hands under any circumstances, we certainly feel better off if the data is unintelligible to the recipient.

The threat tree we have just developed, then, is really a subtree of a threat we can state more completely as: *Other parties obtain __intelligible__ data in cloud.* The top of our tree now looks like this, with 2 conditions that must both be true. The arc connecting the branches indicates an AND relationship.

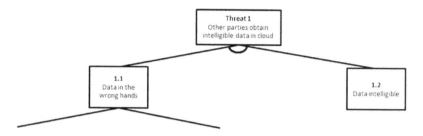

The addition of this second condition is crucial, for two reasons. First, failing to consider all of the aspects in a threat model may give you a false sense of security when you haven't examined all of the angles. More importantly, though, this second condition is something <u>we can easily do something about</u> by having our application encrypt the data it stores and transmits. In contrast we didn't have direct control over all of the first branch's mitigations. Let's develop the *data intelligible* side of the tree a bit more. For brevity reasons we'll just go to one more level, then stop and add mitigations.

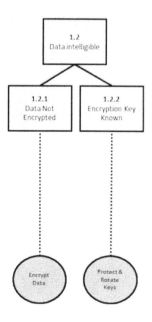

Mitigation is much easier in this subtree because data encryption is in the control of the business. The business merely needs to decide to encrypt, do it well, and protect and rotate its keys. Whenever you can directly mitigate rather than depending on another party to do the right thing you're in a much better position. The full tree that we've developed so far now looks like this.

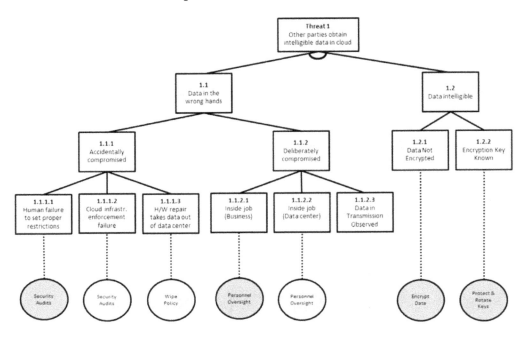

Since the *data intelligible* and *data in the wrong hands* conditions must both be true for this threat to be material, mitigating just one branch mitigates the entire threat. That doesn't mean you should ignore the other branch, but it does mean one of the branches is likely superior in terms of your ability to defend against it. This may enable you to identify a branch as the *critical mitigation path* to focus on.

While this example is not completely developed it should illustrate the spirit of the technique and you can find plenty of reference materials for threat modeling online at MSDN. Cloud security will continue to be a hot topic, and the best way to get a comfort level is to get specific about attacks and defenses. Threat modeling is a good way to do exactly that.

CHAPTER SUMMARY

In this chapter we reviewed the envisioning process, a necessary conversation between decision makers to help an organization realize where its synergies are with cloud computing and Windows Azure. Envisioning should include a benefits discussion, a risk discussion, and identification of opportunities.

Benefit discussions should start with the broad value proposition of Windows Azure and narrow in on the specific benefits that resonate strongly with the company or individual departments. Candidate opportunities for cloud computing will likely arise out of this discussion and should be captured for analysis.

Risk discussions need to address both general and specific security concerns, whether genuine or perceived. Organizational policies for governance, risk management, and compliance must be satisfied as well as regulations imposed externally by government or industry. Security and risk management are best approached as a partnership between the cloud provider and the customer, each with specific responsibilities. Threat modeling is a useful technique for analyzing security threats and other risks that helps uncover areas of vulnerability so that appropriate defenses can be designed.

6

IDENTIFYING OPPORTUNITIES

"Watson, look up at the sky and tell me what you see."
—*Sherlock Holmes*

Some applications and organizational objectives fit cloud computing and the Windows Azure platform well and some do not. This chapter is a catalog of patterns and anti-patterns that can help you swiftly identify candidates and non-candidates even if you are surveying a large portfolio of IT assets. Of course, candidates are only that: candidates. Business and technical analysis is necessary to make ultimate determinations of suitability. We'll look at the following:

- Which scenarios are a good fit for Windows Azure?
- Which scenarios are a poor fit for Windows Azure?

SCENARIOS

Scenarios help simplify the task of surveying your IT assets to find candidates for cloud computing. Each of the scenarios listed below is rated according to the following legend which indicates how good a fit it is for Windows Azure.

● Strong Fit   ◉ Good Fit   ⊙ Poor Fit   ○ Not a Fit

The scenarios are organized by consideration. Note that these considerations are orthogonal: more than one can apply, and it is possible to match positive scenarios and negative scenarios at the same time. For example, an organization that wishes to reduce its data center and move public web sites to the cloud scores as a good fit but those applications requiring a non-Windows operating system are a poor fit:

Example Scenario Rating

Application Deployment Location	Perimeter Network (DMZ)	●	Good Fit
Data Center Objectives	Reduce data center	●	Good Fit
Operating System	Windows	●	Good Fit
Operating System	Linux	○	Not a Fit

Once you've generated the list of candidates you can qualify them through application profiling and TCO/ROI analysis as described in subsequent chapters. Be sure to consider the full picture. Some hurdles may be worth overcoming if there are enough benefits to be realized from other considerations.

Category	Indicators
Application Deployment Location	● Neutral location ("Switzerland") ● Perimeter network / DMZ ◉ Traditional hosting
Application Usage Pattern	● Growing ● Declining ● Seasonal ● Burst ● On/Off ● Unpredictable ◉ Flat
Culture of Risk/Reward	● Aggressive innovator ◉ Pragmatic adopter ⊙ Risk-averse
Data Center Objectives	● Reduce data center ● At or near capacity ● Long-term capacity concerns ● Overflow need ● DR failover need
Data Needs	● Data aggregation ● Low-cost storage ● Data archiving ● Online archive ● Media serving ● Buy reference data ● Sell reference data ● Backup and data replication
Environment Needs	● Production environment ● Staging environment ● QA environment ● Load test environment ● Development environment ○ Non-Windows environment
Financial Preferences	● OpEx preferred to CapEx

Category	Indicators
Hardware Requirements	○ Hardware specs not met by Windows Azure ○ High-performance hardware requirements ○ Specialized hardware requirements
IT Culture	● Strategic leader ● Servant attitude ⊙ Resistant to change / "not invented here"
IT Maturity	● Not adept at IT ● Overloaded IT ● IT reduction objectives
Lifetime	● Start-up ● Experimental ● Uncertain ● Long-running / core to business ⊙ Nearing end of life
Massive Scale	● Massive compute ● Massive data
Operating System	● Windows ○ Other
Product Dependencies	● No local storage requirement ● Designed for Windows Azure ○ Requires local disk persistence ○ Requires access to file shares ○ Requires network access to other machines ○ Not stateless / farm-ready
Service Level Agreement	● 99.9% availability satisfactory ○ 99.9% availability not satisfactory ○ SLA requirements not met by Windows Azure
Stateful Applications	○ In-process state ⊙ Load balancer client-affinity requirement
Technology Platform	● Runs on Windows ● Uses Microsoft tools and technologies
Virtual Network Integration	○ Low latency requirements ○ Integration to non-Windows machines

Application Deployment Location

- Neutral location ("Switzerland")
- Perimeter network / DMZ
- Traditional hosting

● Neutral Location

Some solutions may require or benefit from a neutral location, such as an industry exchange or Business-to-Business sharing of applications, data, or messages. The cloud is the perfect place for cross-organizational integration. I call this "the Switzerland pattern".

● Perimeter Network / DMZ

An application in the perimeter network (DMZ) is a strong candidate for Windows Azure since it is already exposed publicly and any connections needed to internal systems have already been plumbed.

● Traditional Hosting

If an application is being hosted already, it will be easier to move to the Windows Azure platform: it has already been removed from your domain and has a certain level of portability.

Application Usage Pattern

- Growing
- Declining
- Seasonal
- Burst
- On/Off
- Unpredictable
- ⊙ Flat

● Shifting Workloads

The cloud is more cost-effective for shifting workloads such as growing, declining seasonal, burst, on/off, and unpredictable usage patterns. The more interesting the shape of usage pattern, the more cost effective the cloud will be.

○ Flat, Unchanging Workloads

Usage pattern isn't a useful indicator for flat, unchanging workloads. Other factors should be considered to determine suitability for the cloud.

Culture of Risk/Reward

● Aggressive innovator
◒ Pragmatic adopter
⊙ Risk-averse

● Aggressive Innovator

An aggressive innovator is an organization that values reward over risk: they are highly interested in the value of cloud computing and less concerned about risk. They are willing to tolerate and manage risk in order to get reward. These organizations are likely to take the initiative in investigating cloud computing.

◒ Pragmatic Adopter

A pragmatic adopter is an organization that balances risk against reward equally. They are willing to tolerate a certain amount of risk if the reward is great enough to warrant it. They will likely respond well to the Windows Azure value proposition.

⊙ Risk-averse

A risk-averse organization may not be able to get past a certain amount of risk regardless of what the potential reward may be. Low-risk uses of Windows Azure at the onset might be necessary until a comfort level forms from a series of successes.

Data Center Objectives

- At or near capacity
- Overflow need
- Long-term capacity concerns
- DR failover need

● Reduce Data Center

Objectives to reduce data center size align well with Windows Azure. The data center can shift some of its assets over to the cloud.

● At or Near Capacity

The data center is at its limit or close to it and there are imminent capacity concerns. If there is no budget or inclination to expand the data center, Windows Azure can provide the extra capacity needed.

● Long-Term Capacity Concerns

Future capacity needs may outstrip what the data center can support. The data center can be extended into the cloud, where there is plenty of capacity on tap.

● Overflow Need

The data center is generally adequate but at peak times an overflow data center is needed. Using the cloud rather than leasing or creating a second data center is more economical since its use is occasional.

● Disaster Recovery Failover

There is dissatisfaction with current DR arrangements or there are no existing arrangements. A data center is needed to fail over to for disaster recovery. Windows Azure can be the DR data center.

Data Needs

- Data aggregation
- Low-cost storage
- Data archiving
- Online archive
- Media serving
- Buy reference data
- Sell reference data
- Backup / DR

● Data Aggregation

There is a need for data aggregation across departments or companies. The cloud provides an easy way to allocate storage for aggregated data and hosting for data access applications.

● Low-Cost Storage

There is a need for low-cost storage of data. At $0.15/GB/month, Windows Azure Storage is very affordable.

● Data Archiving

You can archive older data to Windows Azure Storage which is reliable and very inexpensive. This can be a good strategy for file data as well as for data that was originally stored in other forms such as a relational database.

● Online Content / Media Serving

There is a need to store content for online access. Windows Azure Storage is a good choice for serving up content: it provides reliable, inexpensive storage that can be served up over the web as media (images, audio, or video) or documents. Even adaptive streaming video can be supported with this approach. Add the Content Distribution Network for global performance caching.

● Buy Reference Data

Companies that purchase reference data may find what they need in the DataMarket service, offered as a subscription.

● Sell Reference Data

Companies seeking an outlet to re-sell data can do so with the DataMarket service. The seller has full control over the terms of use.

● Backup & Data Replication

There is a need for an off-premise location for data backups or to hold replicated data sets for failover. Windows Azure Storage or SQL Azure Database can serve as data repositories.

Hardware Requirements

○ Hardware specs not met by Windows Azure
○ High-performance hardware requirements
○ Specialized hardware requirements

○ Hardware Specifications Not Met by Windows Azure

If your hardware specification requirements exceed what Windows Azure provides you won't be able to use the platform. Windows Azure runs commodity hardware to keep prices low.

○ High-Performance/Specialized Hardware Requirements

If you require high-performance or specialized hardware that differs from what runs in Windows Azure data centers you won't be able to use the platform. Consider whether use of parallelism in Windows Azure might yield acceptable results.

Environment Needs

- ● Production environment
- ● Staging environment
- ● QA environment
- ● Load test environment
- ● Development environment
- ○ Non-Windows environment

● Production Environments

A reliable, scalable, and cost effective production environment is needed. Windows Azure makes for a superb production environment with elastic services for compute, storage, relational data, communication, security, and networking.

● Temporary Environments

You need to create an environment for development, QA, load testing, or staging for a certain amount of time. Windows Azure is suitable for this because the environment can be spun up, adjusted in size, and spun down at a moment's notice. Since development and QA environments often use mock data, there are typically no data sensitivity concerns.

Financial Preferences

- ● OpEx preferred to CapEx

● OpEx Preferred to CapEx

If operational expenditures are preferred to capital expenditures, using the cloud is attractive because up-front server purchases are replaced by a monthly bill for service consumption. This may be easier money to come by.

Industry

Nearly any organization can benefit from cloud computing but some industries have an extra level of synergy:

- Insurance
- Life sciences
- Film/animation
- Utilities

Insurance

Actuarial analysis can involve hundreds of servers. In the cloud, you can "lease" those servers temporarily then discard them when the job is done.

Life Sciences

Human genome processing can involve significant parallel processing or grid computing on large datasets. Windows Azure provides a great foundation for grid computing. Computing and storage resources can be effortlessly allocated and as easily released when no longer needed.

Film / Animation

Film rendering can involve armies of hundreds of servers generating frames. In the cloud, you can "lease" those servers cost effectively and discard them when no longer needed.

Utilities

A utility provider of electricity, water, gas, etc. will "get" the cloud in a special way because they themselves provide a consumption-oriented service with pay-for-what-you-use pricing.

IT Culture

- Strategic leader
- Servant attitude
- ⊙ Resistant to change / "not invented here"

● Strategic Leader

Some IT departments lead the way in bringing strategic new technologies into the company. They regularly investigate and champion new ways to improve the bottom line and improve corporate agility. This kind of IT department will recognize the potential importance of cloud computing and will readily investigate it.

● Servant Attitude

Some IT departments provide little or no resistance to new technologies if they have the backing of business management. IT is there to serve the company, is not political about its own interests, and follows the lead of business decision makers with little pushback. Business interest in the cloud can drive IT adoption of the cloud.

⊙ Resistant to change / "not invented here"

Some IT departments are resistant to change, or to ideas brought in from the outside. Cloud computing may be a hard sell to this kind of IT department. Experimentation with cloud computing by individuals and departments in the company can cause it to be taken seriously by IT. Interest and pressure from senior business management can as well.

IT Maturity

- Not adept at IT
- Overloaded IT
- IT reduction objectives

● Not Adept at IT

For lightweight IT departments that do not have strong expertise, Windows Azure can provide essential capabilities that are hard to achieve locally: scalability, high availability, and reliability.

● Overloaded IT

IT is unable to keep up with demand and is the bottleneck in corporate execution. There is widespread dissatisfaction with IT responsiveness. In the cloud, IT tasks can happen quickly and can be initiated not only by IT but also by departments/individuals across the company.

● IT Reduction

If an IT reduction in staff or budget has recently occurred or is planned, the cloud is a way to save on management and labor costs for certain IT operations.

Lifetime

- Start-up
- Experimental
- Uncertain
- Long-running / core to business
- ⊙ Nearing end of life

● Start-ups & Experimental Initiatives

The cloud is an ideal place for a new business or a new/experimental initiative of an established company. Start-ups need to "scale fast or fail fast". Their degree of success and longevity is unknown. New and experimental initiatives are much like start-ups: their degree of success and longevity is also unknown. The cloud lets you get in and out easily. You can stay in as long as you want and go as big as you want. You can also pull the plug and walk away with no financial or legal commitments beyond the current monthly bill.

● Uncertain Lifetime

Some applications have an uncertain lifetime, such as a hurricane relief site. The cloud lets you set up shop overnight, stay for as long as needed, and walk away cleanly when done.

● Long Running / Core to Business

Long-running applications, such as those core to the business, often provide the greatest return on investment in moving to the cloud because the monthly savings is multiplied by a long lifespan.

⊙ Nearing End of Life

Applications nearing end of life are probably not worth the expense of migrating to the cloud. An exception can be argued in the case of moving non-essential applications off-premise in order to make room for other applications.

Massive Scale

● Massive compute
● Massive data

● Massive Compute

There is a need for dozens, hundreds, or thousands of servers. Windows Azure Compute provides the elastic environment to allocate compute resource at these levels on demand.

● Massive Data

Data needs are in the range of petabytes, terabytes, or hundreds of gigabytes. At a sufficiently extreme level of scale the relational database approach falters and there is a need to use more primitive forms of storage. Windows Azure Storage is a first-rate environment for large-scale data.

Operating System

● Windows
○ Non-Windows Operating System

● Windows

Windows Azure Compute runs Windows Server 2008 / 2008 R2. Applications that already run on these operating systems will be the easiest to migrate. Applications compatible with other versions of Windows should be straightforward to migrate.

○ Non-Windows Operating System

An application can only be hosted in the Windows Azure Compute environment if it is compatible with Windows Server 2008. However, any OS can be used to access cloud services externally such as Windows Azure Storage.

Product Dependencies

● No local storage requirement
● Designed for Windows Azure
○ Requires local disk persistence
○ Requires access to file shares
○ Requires network access to other machines
○ Not stateless / farm-ready

○ Cloud-Contrary Product Characteristics

Enterprise server products are poor fits to run in the cloud if any of the following are true, unless source code is available for modification.

- The product requires persistent local disk (a cloud VM instance's disk is not guaranteed).
- The product requires read/write access to a file share (Windows Azure has blob storage but not file shares). There is the Windows Azure drive feature which can map a blob to a local drive letter, but this feature is very limited on the write side and is best suited for read-only uses.
- The product requires direct network access to other machines (Windows Azure isolates VM instances on the network).
- The product is not designed to run in a stateless server farm configuration (a single instance doesn't have high availability).

Service Level Agreement

● Windows Azure availability satisfactory
○ Windows Azure availability not satisfactory
○ SLA requirements not met by Windows Azure

● Windows Azure Availability Satisfactory

The Windows Azure SLA of 99.95% for Compute and 99.9% for most other services is satisfactory, meeting or exceeding availability requirements.

○ Windows Azure Availability Not Satisfactory

The Windows Azure SLA does not meet availability requirements.

○ Other SLA Requirements

If an SLA requirement has other stipulations beyond availability, they may not be provided by Windows Azure. For example, Recovery Time Objective (RTO) and Recovery Point Objective (RPO) are not part of the Windows Azure SLA. If the platform does not provide a needed SLA requirement, consider whether your application can provide it.

Stateful Applications

⊙ In-process state
⊙ Load balancer client affinity requirement

⊙ In-Process State

In-process state is not a useful approach in the cloud because each client request can be sent to any VM instance, and VM instances are not guaranteed to be persistent.

⊙ Load Balancer Client Affinity Requirement

Windows Azure load-balanced endpoints do not provide any kind of client stickiness; each request can go to any VM instance. Applications requiring client affinity will not work as-is in the cloud. Note: it is possible to implement client-instance affinity by creating your own intermediary software layer—at added hosting cost.

Technology Platform

● Runs on Windows
● Uses Microsoft tools and technologies

● Runs on Windows

Applications that run on the Windows operating system are much easier to migrate to Windows Azure than applications targeting other operating system.

● Uses Microsoft Tools and Technologies

Microsoft operating systems, products and technologies are used. While it's not a requirement to be a "Microsoft shop" in order to use Windows Azure, it does streamline the migration process if you're using Windows Server, SQL Server, the .NET Framework, ASP.NET, Silverlight, or WCF.

Virtual Network Integration / Hybrid Cloud

○ VPN latency not acceptable
○ Integration to non-Windows machines

⊙ Low Latency Requirements

The Windows Azure Connect virtual networking feature allows cloud assets to access local assets. For scenarios requiring low latency, performance over a VPN connection may not be satisfactory. Performance testing is encouraged.

○ Non-Windows Integrations

The Windows Azure Connect virtual networking feature only allows Windows-based machines to be linked. Non-Windows machines cannot participate.

CHAPTER SUMMARY

In this chapter we looked at a catalog of scenarios, rated to indicate their fitness for Windows Azure. These patterns and anti-patterns should only be used to make tentative conclusions: the short list of candidates then needs to be thoroughly analyzed from business and technical perspectives. When surveying a large IT portfolio, these patterns can help you consider applications in groups for faster initial findings.

7

PROFILING APPLICATIONS

""Let us hear the suspicions. I will look after the proofs."
—Sherlock Holmes

Applications, like people, are complex entities with many different attributes. In order to determine how good a fit an application is for cloud computing with Windows Azure, you'll need to consider it from multiple angles and then come to an overall conclusion. We'll look at the following:

- How do you profile an application?
- How can an application be scored for suitability?
- How should suitability scores be used?

CREATING AN APPLICATION INVENTORY

An application inventory is a record of information and analysis about applications you are considering for cloud computing. Whether you plan to survey your entire portfolio of IT assets or are just focused on one or two leading candidates, the same questions need to be asked about any application you are seriously considering for the Windows Azure platform.

Surveying a Large Portfolio

If you are surveying a large number of applications, it may be impractical to perform a deep analysis on each of them. A useful technique is to group your applications by common characteristics and determine which groups are worthy of inspection. A good way to group your applications is to use one or more of the patterns in Chapter 6.

For example, imagine you have dozens of applications and can divide them into 3 large groups: public-facing web applications, internal-facing departmental applications, and mainframe applications. From this information alone we can discern where to focus our efforts. Public-facing web applications are low hanging fruit for migration to the cloud and should be the first group to receive our attention. Departmental applications should be studied next: they can also be good candidates for the cloud but may require extra work to support domain authentication and integrations to external systems. We can skip study of the mainframe applications as they could not run in the cloud.

Creating an Application Profile

An application profile captures the essential characteristics of an application at a glance. It should convey the business context of the application as well as technical information. To form a base profile for an application, collect the following information, plus anything else that might be useful to your decision-making process.

Application Name	
Used by	
Access methods	
Business Value	
Lifecycle stage	
Remaining lifetime	
No. total users	
No. concurrent users	
No. servers	
Server specs	
Database data (GB)	
Non-database data (GB)	
SLA requirements	
Usage pattern	
Size / complexity	
Platform	

Below is a sample application profile.

Application Name	Health Access Plus
Used by	The public and by customers
Access methods	Web and mobile
Business Value	This app is a differentiator for us. It contributes to our reputation for technical innovation and ease of access to information without bureaucracy. It's core to our business advantage.
Lifecycle stage	In production
Remaining lifetime	5+ years
No. total users	10000
No. concurrent users	500
No. servers	4
Server specs	Similar specs to Windows Azure VM Large size
Database data (GB)	25
Non-database data (GB)	2 (file storage)
SLA requirements	Availability: 3 9's. Recovery: RTO of 30 min / RPO of 4 hours
Usage pattern	Increasing
Size / complexity	Medium
Platform	Microsoft – Windows, .NET Framework

DOWNLOAD: You can download a worksheet for capturing application profiles from http://AzureHandbook.com (specify download code 145657471X).

SCORING SUITABILITY

Once an application has been profiled, proceed to examine it from multiple perspectives and score each for suitability. Include these considerations:

- Platform Alignment
- Ease of Code Migration
- Ease of Data Migration
- Savings
- Access Method
- Usage Pattern
- Life Expectancy
- SLA Requirement
- Integration Points
- Data Sensitivity
- Policy Barriers
- Regulatory Barriers

You can score each area on a scale. Once you've scored these individual areas, you can integrate the results and an overall suitability score can be computed. There are two ways you can use this score: first, if the score is very high or very low that will make a strong statement about whether the candidate is viable; second, you can use scores to rank candidate applications relative to each other.

There are a variety of approaches and tools you could use to gather and score suitability; I'm going to describe the suitability model we came up with at Neudesic which was designed with Windows Azure in mind. We'll use a scale of 0.0-5.0, where 5.0 is highly suitable for Windows Azure and 0.0 is highly unsuitable. For some categories the scoring will be very polar (0.0 or 5.0 with little middle ground) but for others there will be a granular spread. Regardless of composite scores, any individual score that is extremely low (0.0-1.0) probably represents a show-stopper; if you can't get around that obstacle, the other scores don't matter no matter how high they may be.

Suitability scoring is valuable but it needs to be thought of as an insightful exercise rather than a deterministic process. It doesn't replace human judgment but does provide helpful information from which to make informed decisions. The categories and scoring guidelines presented here should work well for most organizations, but you should feel free to tinker with the suitability categories and weight the scoring system to reflect what's important to your organization.

Consideration	Score
Platform Alignment	
Ease of Code Migration	
Ease of Data Migration	
Savings	
Access Method	
Usage Pattern	
Life Expectancy	
SLA Requirement	
Integration Points	
Data Sensitivity	
Policy Barriers	
Regulatory Barriers	
Overall Suitability Score	

Platform Alignment

Platform Alignment measures how well the application's software dependencies can be matched in the cloud. "Platform" includes all software the application depends on, including operating system, frameworks, libraries, services, and products. Score the layers individually using the scale below and then take the lowest score of the group as your platform alignment score.

Platform Alignment Scoring Guidelines

Score	Guideline
5.0	Fully compatible
4.0	Can be easily migrated
3.0	Can be migrated with moderate difficulty / expense
2.0	Can be migrated with high difficulty / expense
1.0	Requires complete substitution or port of a software layer
0.0	Inherently not compatible

Score platform alignment highly if all of the application's platform requirements can be satisfied by any of the following:

- Windows Azure Compute intrinsic stack (Windows Server, .NET 3.5/4.0)
- Software that can be installed on top of Windows Azure Compute
- Platform services such as SQL Azure Database

In Example 1 below the application is a good fit for Windows Azure: the operating system is a match; SQL Azure Database can replace SQL Server; and upgrading the .NET framework to a later version is usually very straightforward.

Example 1: Platform Alignment Score 4.0 (Good Fit)

Platform	Score	Comments
Windows Operating System	5.0	Supported on Azure
SQL Server Database	5.0	Can use SQL Azure Database
.NET Framework 2.0	4.0	Needs to be 3.5+ but easy to update

In Example 2 we have a clear non-fit: none of the application's platform requirements are practical for Windows Azure. Migration of this application would amount to rewriting it.

Example 2: Platform Alignment Score 0.0 (Non-Fit)

Platform	Score	Comments
Linux Operating System	0.0	Not available in Windows Azure
Oracle Database	0.0	Not feasible to run in Windows Azure
Sun Grid Engine	1.0	Challenging to run in Windows Azure

Ease of Code Migration

Ease of Code Migration measures the level of effort needed to make the application code compatible with Windows Azure Compute. All executable code should be considered, including: client and server code; presentation code; web service code; and back-end code. Score each tier of your solution that has executable code using the scale below and take the average as your score. If some tiers are significantly larger than others you can use weighed scoring.

Ease of Code Migration Scoring Guidelines

Score	Guideline
5.0	No code changes required
4.0	Code changes are minor
3.0	Code changes are moderate
2.0	Code changes are significant
1.0	Code changes are unacceptably expensive, complex, or risky
0.0	Code changes are not possible

Score ease of code migration highly if there is little to change and your development team is highly confident that the changes are straightforward and low risk.

In Example 1 below the application code requires only the most minor of changes, yielding a high score.

Example 1: Ease of Code Migration Score 4.5 (Very Good Fit)

Code Tier	Score	Comments
ASP.NET Web Site	4.5	Only change is session state provider
SQL Server Database	5.0	Can use SQL Azure Database, no changes

In Example 2 we have a questionable fit: although Java applications and the Tomcat web runtime can be run in Windows Azure, this scenario has a dependency on many Java libraries that have not been ported to Windows Azure, making for a large set of unknowns.

Example 2: Ease of Code Migration Score 2.5 (Questionable Fit)

Code Tier	Score	Comments
Java Application	1.0	Uses a large number of Java libraries
Tomcat Runtime	4.0	Can run in Windows Azure

Ease of Data Migration

Ease of Data Migration measures the level of effort needed to move the application data to Windows Azure. All application data should be considered, whether destined for the SQL Azure Database, Windows Azure Storage, or some other storage destination. If you have multiple data stores, score each data store and take the average as your score. If some data stores are significantly larger than others you can use weighed scoring.

Ease of Data Migration Scoring Guidelines

Score	Guideline
5.0	No data changes are necessary
4.0	Data changes are minor
3.0	Data changes are moderate
2.0	Data changes are significant
1.0	Data changes are unacceptably expensive, complex, or risky
0.0	Data changes are not possible

Score ease of data migration highly if the data to migrate easily fits a cloud data service. Impose a lower score if data exceeds a size limit (requiring partitioning) or if there are feature gaps between the original form of storage and the destination in the cloud (requiring compensatory code changes). Also include processing closely tied to data, such as stored procedures, reporting, analysis services, and synchronization.

In Example 1 below the application data requires very few changes, yielding a high score.

Example 1: Ease of Data Migration Score 4.5 (Very Good Fit)

Code Tier	Score	Comments
SQL Server Database	5.0	Can use SQL Azure Database, no changes
File Storage	4.0	Can use Windows Azure blob storage; minor code changes needed to access blobs rather than files

In Example 2 we have a poor fit: although it is often easy to migrate SQL Server databases to SQL Azure Database, in this example there are feature disconnects which would require reimplementation of some parts of the application. The original application also uses more than just core database services and requires reporting and analysis capabilities; as of this writing, SQL Azure Reporting is only in CTP and there is no SQL Server Analysis Services counterpart in the cloud yet.

Example 2: Ease of Data Migration Score 2.0 (Poor Fit)

Code Tier	Score	Comments
SQL Server 2005 Database	2.0	Heavy use of full-text search and XML indexing, features not available in SQL Azure
SQL Server Reporting Services	4.0	Easily switch to SQL Azure Reporting but not yet commercially available
SQL Server Analysis Services	0.0	Not yet available in Windows Azure

Savings

Savings measures the significance of savings as compared to leaving the application on-premise. If you are able to compute a Return on Investment (described in Chapter 8), you will arrive at two figures: a monthly savings and an overall savings for the expected lifetime of the application. Use this latter value to arrive at a score using the table below. If you're unable to make an ROI determination, use a "neutral" score of 2.5.

Savings Scoring Guidelines

Score	Guideline
5.0	Savings of $100,000 or more
4.0	Savings of $50,000 or more
3.0	Savings of $10,000 or more
2.0	Savings of $5,000 or more
1.0	Savings of $1,000 or more
0.0	No savings

Different companies have varying views of how much savings is considered significant. Change the scoring scale if you wish but score all applications with a consistent measurement.

In Example 1 below the application data requires very few changes, yielding a high score.

Example 1: Savings Score 5.0 (Very Good Fit)

ROI	Score	Comments
$4000 saved per month. Application lifetime of 5 years. Total ROI of $234,000 after subtracting migration costs.	5.0	Significant savings

In Example 2 we have a poor fit: the monthly savings is low and the overall lifetime of the application is uncertain.

Example 2: Saving Score 1.0 (Poor Fit)

Total Lifetime ROI	Score	Comments
$100 saved per month. Application lifetime unknown. Total ROI unknown.	1.0	Savings is trivial

Access Method

Access Method measures how viable the application's method(s) of access are in the cloud.

Access Method Scoring Guidelines

Score	Guideline
5.0	Access methods have direct counterparts in the cloud
4.0	Access methods can be made to work in the cloud with minor changes
3.0	Access methods can be made to work in the cloud with moderate changes
2.0	Access methods can be made to work in the cloud with significant changes
1.0	Access methods unacceptably expensive or impractical to achieve in cloud
0.0	Access methods are inherently not compatible with the cloud

Score highly if the application easily fits the cloud: web sites, RIA applications, web services, or background/batch processing. Assign a low score for access methods that are difficult, impractical, or impossible to implement in the cloud today: desktop, virtual desktop, and terminal serving. Assign a medium score for virtual network connections, and fine-tune the score based on whether you believe the reliability and latency will be acceptable for your needs.

In Example 1 below the application is a good fit for Windows Azure: the application has a web site interface, easily achieved in the cloud with a Windows Azure Compute web role.

Example 1: Access Method Score 5.0 (Very Good Fit)

Access Method	Score	Comments
Web site	5.0	Windows Azure Compute web role

In Example 2 we have a clear non-fit: the application is made for a terminal server connection and it is not currently viable to host that in Windows Azure.

Example 2: Access Method Score 0.0 (Non-Fit)

Access Method	Score	Comments
Terminal Server Connection	0.0	Not possible in Windows Azure today

Usage Pattern

Usage Pattern measures how strongly the application's usage pattern leverages cloud computing's on-demand, elastic nature.

Usage Pattern Scoring Guidelines

Score	Guideline
5.0	Seasonal, cyclic, on/off, or burst usage pattern
4.0	Increasing or decreasing usage pattern
3.0	Unpredictable usage pattern
2.5	Flat, unchanging usage pattern
1.0	Usage pattern difficult to achieve reliably in the cloud
0.0	Usage pattern not possible in the cloud

Score highly if the usage pattern has an interesting shape: increasing, decreasing, on/off, burst, seasonal, cyclic, or unpredictable. Score neutral on the scale if the usage pattern is flat. Assign a low score if the usage pattern can't be achieved well or at all in the cloud, such as is the case with some real-time and high-performance computing applications where the hardware or throughput requirements may exceed what the platform provides.

In Example 1 below the usage pattern is seasonal, a strong fit for Windows Azure: the business is a tax preparation service that needs much more computing power in March and April than the rest of the year.

Example 1: Usage Pattern Score 5.0 (Neutral)

Usage Pattern	Score	Comments
Seasonal	5.0	Need much more capacity in March-April

In Example 2 we have a neutral fit: the application has a flat, stable usage pattern. In this scenario usage pattern is not a useful indicator of whether the application makes sense in the cloud.

Example 2: Usage Pattern Score 2.5 (Neutral)

Access Method	Score	Comments
Flat	2.5	Usage pattern not a determining factor

Life Expectancy

Life Expectancy measures how much remaining life is expected for the application. If lifetime is uncertain, the cloud is a good choice because it is easy to jump in and jump out without making commitments. If lifetime is long, it will strengthen the return on the costs of migrating to the cloud.

Life Expectancy Scoring Guidelines

Score	Guideline
5.0	5 years or more
4.0	4 years or more, or uncertain lifetime
3.0	3 years or more
2.0	2 years or more
1.0	1 year or more
0.0	Less than 1 year

Score highly if the application is expected to be in use for 5 years or more (this will often be the case when an application is core to the business). Assign a neutral score to an expected lifetime of 3 years. Assign a low score for applications that will be used for a year or less.

In Example 1 below the life expectancy is over 10 years: the application is core to the organization and they expect to use it for as long as they are in business.

Example 1: Life Expectancy Score 5.0 (Very Good Fit)

Life Expectancy	Score	Comments
10+ years	5.0	App is core to the business

In Example 2 the application is declining and use is expected to be completely decommissioned in a year. This application is likely not worth migrating to the cloud.

Example 2: Life Expectancy Score 2.0 (Poor)

Life Expectancy	Score	Comments
12 months	1.0	Difficult to justify migrating to cloud

Service Level Agreement (SLA)

A Service Level Agreement is a contract between a business and its IT department/provider about expectations and commitment to a certain level of service. The *SLA* score measures how well a desired SLA can be matched in the cloud.

The primary SLA measurement Windows Azure commits to is availability which is traditionally measured in 9's. Most services in Windows Azure provide 3 9's of availability (99.9%) and Windows Azure Compute provides 3 and a half 9's (99.95%). For most services you could be looking at 8 hours of unavailability per year. Note that for hosting the SLA only applies if there are at least 2 instances per VM farm.

SLA Scoring Guidelines

Score	Guideline
5.0	Availability requirement of 3 9's or less and no other SLA demands
0.0	Availability requirement in excess of 3 9's or other SLA demands

Score highly if the availability requirement is 3 9's or less. A requirement for higher availability is a show-stopper unless you can get the requirement relaxed. If the business requires an SLA that has other considerations (such as a specific response time or data recovery time) it may not be possible to demonstrate that Windows Azure meets them other than through experimentation. For some services throughput *targets* are documented but this is not the same as an SLA commitment. Some SLA requirements are more in your hands than the cloud and can be accommodated by your application design and processes (for example data recovery time from a disaster). If you have multiple SLA considerations, take the lowest score as your overall SLA score.

In Example 1 below the only SLA requirements is 2 9's availability, which Windows Azure exceeds.

Example 1: SLA Score 5.0 (Very Good fit)

SLA Requirement	Score	Comments
2 9's of availability	5.0	Windows Azure provides more than sufficient availability

In Example 2 we have a fit on SLA from an availability perspective but there is also a demand for a specific response time. As the Windows Azure SLA does not currently include performance commitments, a low score results.

Example 2: SLA Score 0.0 (Poor Fit)

SLA Requirement	Score	Comments
3 9's of availability	5.0	Matches the Windows Azure SLA
Maximum response time of 2 seconds for web requests	0.0	Not an SLA category Windows Azure commits to

Integration Points

Integration Points measures the number of *internal* integrations your application has to other on-premise systems. The greater the number of integrations, the greater the migration cost is likely to be. Public integration points are not a concern here: your application in the cloud will have no problem reaching them. Internal integrations, on the other hand, will require you to put in place some means of accessing these internal systems from the cloud (such as web services or a Windows Azure Connect VPN connection).

Integration Points Scoring Guidelines

Score	Guideline
5.0	No internal integrations, or external integrations
4.0	1 or more internal integrations
3.0	2 or more internal integrations
2.0	3 or more internal integrations
1.0	4 or more internal integrations
0.0	5 or more internal integrations

Only count the integrations that are internal where there is no existing means of external access.

In Example 1 we have a good fit: although the application has 2 integrations, none count as an internal integration: one is a publicly-accessible vendor web service and the other already has an external means of access already in place.

Example 1: Integration Points Score 5.0 (Good Fit)

Integrations	Score	Comments
Integration to vendor (external)	(5.0)	Public, not included in score
Integration to ordering system via externally-accessible web service	(5.0)	Externally accessible, not included in score

In Example 2 we have a poor fit: the application has many internal integrations, likely indicating an expensive migration.

Example 2: SLA Score 1.0 (Poor Fit)

Integrations	Score	Comments
CRM System (internal) ERP System (internal) Delivery System (internal) HR System (internal)	1.0	4 integrations to accommodate

Data Sensitivity

Data Sensitivity measures the sensitivity you attach to your data and willingness to take it off premise. Data can be considered sensitive for many reasons, including proprietary value to the company and the responsibility to safeguard private information.

Data Sensitivity Scoring Guidelines

Score	Guideline
5.0	No concerns about data in the cloud
3.0	Data may go into the cloud if it can be demonstrated to be secure
0.0	Unwilling to permit data to go off-premise under any circumstances

Score high when there is little concern about data sensitivity and low when data is not permitted to go in the cloud under any circumstances (a show-stopper unless you can get the decision reversed). Take the lowest score as your overall score.

In Example 1 we have a good fit: there are no firm objections to data being in the cloud as long as it is reasonably secured.

Example 1: Data Sensitivity Score 4.0 (Good Fit)

Data & Data Sensitivity	Score	Comments
User profiles - private	4.0	Allowed in the cloud if secured
Property images - public	5.0	Allowed in the cloud

In Example 2 we have a non-fit: some application data is forbidden to go off-premise.

Example 2: Data Sensitivity Score 0.0 (Non-Fit)

Data & Data Sensitivity	Score	Comments
Account data – highly sensitive	0.0	Risk management group will not allow data off-premise

Policy Barriers

Policy Barriers measures rules within your organization that stand in the way of moving an application or its data to a cloud computing environment.

Policy Barriers Scoring Guidelines

Score	Guideline
5.0	No policy barriers
4.0	Policies must be satisfied but are only a formality
3.0	Policies must be satisfied that are reasonably straightforward to satisfy
2.0	Policies must be satisfied that are extremely hard to satisfy
1.0	Policies stand in the way of cloud adoption unless they can be waived
0.0	Policies stand in the way of cloud adoption and cannot be challenged

Score high when there are no policy barriers and low when there are implacable barriers.

In Example 1 we have a very good fit: there are no policy barriers in the way of cloud computing adoption.

Example 1: Policy Barriers Score 5.0 (Very Good Fit)

Policy Barriers	Score	Comments
None	5.0	No policy barriers

In Example 2 we have a non-fit: the application is considered too valuable to risk putting in the cloud regardless of how well it is secured, a firm company policy.

Example 2: Policy Barriers Score 0.0 (Non-Fit)

Policy Barriers	Score	Comments
Trading application and data must be kept and used at corporate office (rigid policy)	0.0	Company policy disallows off-premise

Regulatory Barriers

Regulatory Barriers measures regulations imposed on your organization from government or industry that interfere with cloud computing adoption.

Regulatory Barriers Scoring Guidelines

Score	Guideline
5.0	No regulatory barriers
4.0	Regulations must be satisfied but are only a formality
3.0	Regulations must be satisfied that are reasonably straightforward to satisfy
2.0	Regulations must be satisfied that are extremely hard to satisfy
1.0	Regulations stand in the way of cloud adoption unless they can be waived
0.0	Regulations stand in the way of cloud adoption and cannot be challenged

Score high when there are no regulatory barriers and low when there are implacable barriers.

In Example 1 we have a very good fit: there are no regulatory barriers in the way of cloud computing adoption.

Example 1: Regulatory Barriers Score 5.0 (Very Good Fit)

Regulatory Barriers	Score	Comments
None	5.0	No regulatory barriers

In Example 2 we have a poor fit, a PCI DSS certification requirement that Windows Azure does not currently have. It's possible this can be addressed by splitting the application into PCI and non-PCI portions and moving only one part to the cloud.

Example 2: Regulatory Barriers Score 1.0 (Poor-Fit)

Regulatory Barriers	Score	Comments
PCI DSS certification requirement for payment processing	1.0	Windows Azure data centers are not yet certified for PCI DSS

ANALYZING SUITABILITY SCORES

Once you have determined individual suitability scores for an application you can average them to create an overall suitability score. A succinct summary like the one below makes it easy to take in the full suitability story at a glance.

Health Access Plus

Consideration	Score
Platform Alignment	5.0
Ease of Code Migration	4.5
Ease of Data Migration	4.0
Savings	3.5
Access Method	5.0
Usage Pattern	4.0
Life Expectancy	4.0
SLA Requirement	4.5
Integration Points	5.0
Data Sensitivity	5.0
Policy Barriers	5.0
Regulatory Barriers	5.0
Overall Suitability Score	**4.5**

By plotting suitability scores in a radar chart format, application suitability scores can be shown as shapes. This format conveys that many factors have been considered yet it is very approachable to both business and technical people. These shapes can be compared to a desired shape to show their individual suitability. In addition, shapes for multiple applications can be easily compared and ranked for relative suitability.

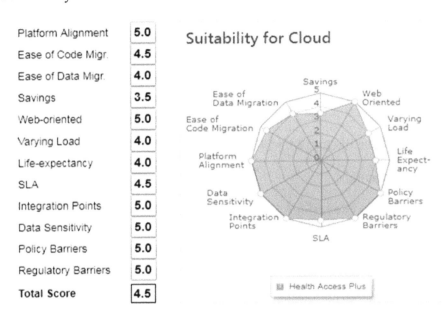

Platform Alignment	5.0
Ease of Code Migr.	4.5
Ease of Data Migr.	4.0
Savings	3.5
Web-oriented	5.0
Varying Load	4.0
Life-expectancy	4.0
SLA	4.5
Integration Points	5.0
Data Sensitivity	5.0
Policy Barriers	5.0
Regulatory Barriers	5.0
Total Score	**4.5**

With suitability scores in place you are now in a position to make informed decisions about what makes sense in the cloud and what doesn't. You can further prioritize your short list of cloud candidates based on relative suitability or a metric you care strongly about (such as savings).

CHAPTER SUMMARY

In this chapter we looked at how to profile applications by studying them from multiple perspectives and arriving at an overall suitability score. We recommended scoring suitability based on Platform Alignment, Ease of Code Migration, Ease of Data Migration, Savings, Access Method, Usage Pattern, Life Expectancy, SLA Requirement, Integration Points, Data Sensitivity, Policy Barriers, and Regulatory Barriers. We saw that suitability scores are useful for determining an individual application's fitness for Windows Azure and also for relative ranking of cloud candidates.

8

ESTIMATING MIGRATION

"Reach for the Sky."
—Woody, in "Toy Story"

Some applications migrate easily to Windows Azure while others may require moderate or significant changes. Migration should begin with a technical analysis in which the extent of architectural, code, and data changes are determined. Once scoped, migration costs can be estimated and factored into the ROI calculation to determine if a migration makes sense. We'll answer these questions:

- How is a migration candidate analyzed?
- How is a migration approach determined?
- How can operational costs be optimized in a migration?
- How is the extent of development work estimated?

OVERVIEW OF MIGRATION ESTIMATION

In order to analyze migration of an existing solution to Windows Azure the following activities should be performed:

Migration Analysis

1. *Analyze the Solution*. Analyze and capture the original solution's software components, technologies, and environment.
2. *Map the solution to the Cloud*. Map each of the solution's software components, technologies, and environmental requirements to Windows Azure. Document the planned approach for each area.
3. *Perform an Operational Cost Analysis*. Determine whether your solution's existing design and behaviors are a good fit for the Windows Azure pricing model. If the solution has high or uncapped cost tendencies, modify your solution design and migration approach to be cost-efficient.
4. *Estimate Tasks*. Estimate the tasks required to move to the cloud. Consider planning, architectural and design changes, code migration, data migration, security, integrations, QA, operations monitoring, and governance.

ANALYZE EXISTING SOLUTION

↓

MAP SOLUTION COMPONENTS TO WINDOWS AZURE

↓

ANALYZE OPERATIONAL COST

↓

SCOPE AND ESTIMATE DEVELOPMENT TASKS

When doing migrations en masse for a large portfolio of IT assets, you'll typically encounter batches of similar applications whose migrations involve similar work. Be on the lookout for patterns: recognizing them will help you get to a point of high velocity in migration work.

To illustrate the process, we'll progressively analyze 2 scenarios as we discuss the activities involved:

- Scenario 1: A corporate web site
- Scenario 2: A departmental application

Often the desire in a migration is to change the existing solution as little as possible to keep costs down. This is different from new application development where you might choose to design for the cloud and more strongly leverage the platform.

DOWNLOAD: You can download a worksheet for migration estimation from http://AzureHandbook.com (specify download code 145657471X).

1 ANALYZING A SOLUTION

It's necessary to understand an existing application's architecture well before you can come to any conclusions about how it will look in the cloud or what the scope of the effort will be. To do this quickly and efficiently, ask questions that bring these 3 areas of information to light:

1. *Software Components*. What are the software tiers and major components of the solution?
2. *Platform*. What technologies and products are used in the solution, and what role do they play?
3. *Environment*. What supporting environment does the solution require, including internal and external systems and security infrastructure?

Software Components

To identify software components, start simply by creating a high level architectural diagram and ascertain the primary tiers or layers of the solution along functional lines. Some of the most common tiers are those listed below, but a solution could certainly have other layers than these, such as a back-end processing tier.

- *Presentation Tier*. The user interface or "front end", which might support one or more of the following access methods: desktop, web, mobile.
- *Business Logic Tier / Web Services Tier / Middle Tier*. A layer between the front-end UI and back-end data containing business and data access logic.
- *Data Tier*. The database or other storage for the application, and supporting interfaces for accessing it.

On the next page, the tiers of our 2 sample solutions are diagrammed. The first is a 3-tier corporate web site that is public on the Internet. The second is a 2-tier departmental application used internally and secured to the company's domain.

Diagramming Solution Tiers

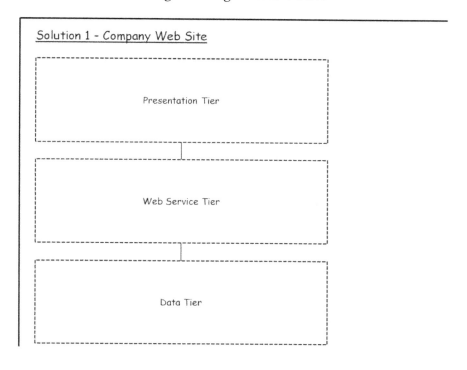

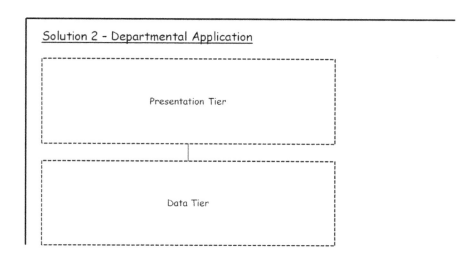

Once the software layers are identified, take the diagram to a more detailed level and also ascertain the software components within each layer. It's important to have sufficient granularity here so that no dependent technologies or products are overlooked in the analysis.

The software components for our two sample scenarios are shown below and diagrammed on the next page. We now have a good idea of what parts make up the solutions and can start to get specific about their technical characteristics.

Solution 1: Company Web Site (3-Tier)

Tier	Component
Presentation Layer	Web Site
	Chart Control
	E-Commerce Control
Web Services Layer	Web Service
Data Layer	Database

Solution 2: Departmental Application (2-Tier)

Tier	Component
Presentation Layer	Web Site
Data Layer	Database

Diagramming Software Components

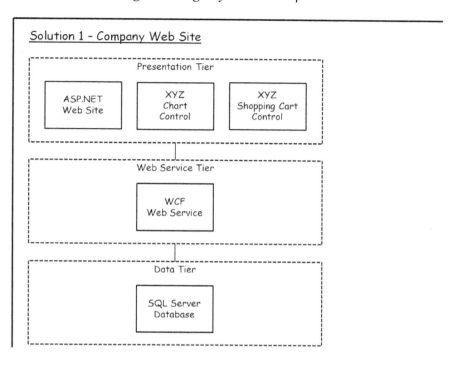

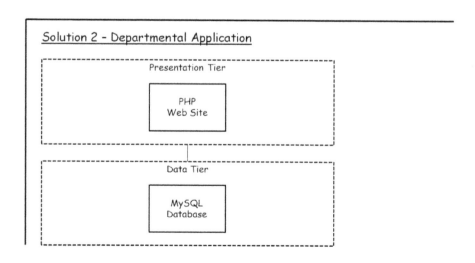

Platform

Once the software tiers and major components are known, inquire what technologies or products are used in each of them. Capture the technologies used by listing them alongside the components identified in the previous step. It's important to be thorough, as we must consider what the correct equivalent in the cloud should be for each.

In our two sample scenarios, we learn that one is based primarily on ASP.NET, WCF, and SQL Server while the other uses PHP and MySQL.

Solution 1: Company Web Site (ASP.NET / WCF / SQL Server)

Tier	Component	Technologies / Products
Presentation Layer	Web Site	ASP.NET, .NET 3.0, CSS, JavaScript, IIS, Windows Server
	Chart Control	XYZ Charts
	Shopping Cart Control	XYZ Cart
Web Services Layer	Web Service	WCF, .NET 3.0, Windows Server
Data Layer	Database	SQL Server 2008, Windows Server

Solution 2: Departmental Application (PHP / MySQL)

Tier	Component	Technologies / Products
Presentation Layer	Web Site	PHP, Apache Tomcat
Data Layer	Database	MySQL

Environment

In addition to understanding the make-up of a solution we must also understand the environment it needs to operate in. There are 2 kinds of environmental attachments to consider:

- Integrations – what other systems does the solution interact with, and which of these are internal vs. external?
- Security – what security infrastructure is needed for the application, for example access to a domain's Active Directory.

In our example scenarios, each has one true environmental requirement. The company web site has an external integration to Bing Maps. It also has a membership database requirement but that is a self-contained part of the solution so we can dismiss it as a concern. The departmental application depends on a domain controller for employee authentication.

Solution 1: Company Web Site Environment

Environmental Need	Type	Location	Notes
Map Integration	Integration	External (Microsoft)	Silverlight map control
Membership Database	Security	Self-contained in solution	Custom username/ password database

Solution 2: Departmental Application Environment

Environmental Need	Type	Location	Notes
Domain Authentication	Security	On-premise	IBM Tivoli

We have now gathered enough information about the solution to define how it can be mapped to Windows Azure.

Solution Diagrams showing Environment

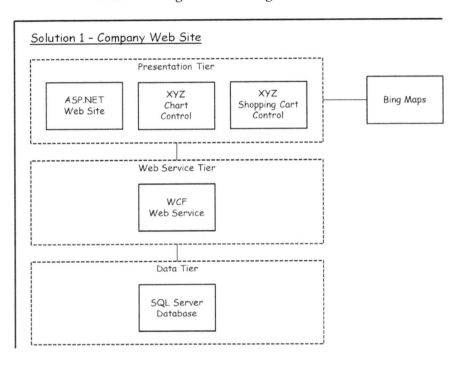

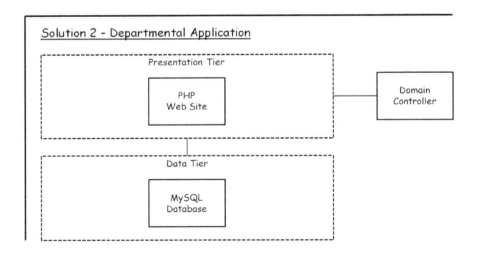

2 MAP THE SOLUTION TO THE CLOUD

In this activity you will map a solution's components, technologies, and environmental requirements to the Windows Azure platform. In each case, you will need to make a finding:

1. *Equivalent*. What the nearest equivalent in the cloud is. In some cases you will have a choice to make among several alternatives.
2. *Delta*. How similar or dissimilar the proposed equivalent is to what is currently being used. Assign one of these values:
    - *Not in Cloud* – the component will not move to the cloud
    - *As Is* – will work in the cloud as is without the need for any changes
    - *Minor* – move to the cloud is very straightforward, changes are minor
    - *Major* – many changes are needed but the approach is retained
    - *Replace/Rewrite* – a reimplementation or substitution is necessary
    - *Future* – requires a future platform feature in order to achieve

In our sample solution scenarios, we see the ASP.NET web site solution maps very cleanly to Windows Azure and very little needs to be changed. The web site and its controls can run as-is in a web role, and the SQL Server 2008 database migrates easily to the SQL Azure Database service. The self-contained membership database moves with the solution. The Bing Maps integration causes no issues because it is universally accessible.

The departmental PHP / MySQL solution requires more in the way of changes. We could continue to run PHP in Tomcat in a worker role, or switch over to IIS in a web role. Since MySQL isn't designed for a cloud computing environment, the best thing to do with the database is migrate it to a SQL Azure Database. The IBM Tivoli domain authentication also poses a challenge. If the solution is to be hosted in the cloud then some external means of authenticating employees will be necessary. A federated security server in the corporate DMZ can be used to achieve this.

Solution 1: Company Web Site Mapping

Tier/Component	Technologies	Mapping	Delta
Presentation Layer			
Web Site	ASP.NET, CSS, JavaScript	Same - web role	As Is
Chart Control	XYZ Charts	Same - web role	As Is
Shopping Cart Control	XYZ Chart	Same - web role	As Is
Web Services Layer			
WCF Services	IIS, WCF, ADO.NET	Same - web role	As Is
Data Layer			
Database	SQL Server 2008	SQL Azure	Minor
Environment			
Bing Maps	Silverlight control	Same – web role	As is

Solution 2: Departmental Solution Mapping

Tier/Component	Technologies	Mapping	Delta
Presentation Layer			
Web Site	PHP	Same - web role	As Is
Data Layer			
Database	MySQL	SQL Azure	Major
Environment			
Domain security	IBM Tivoli	Federated security server (DMZ)	Major

Solutions Mapped to the Windows Azure Platform

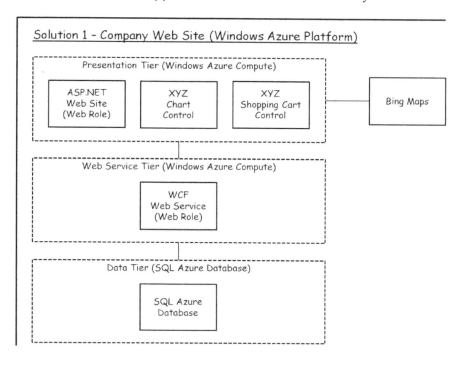

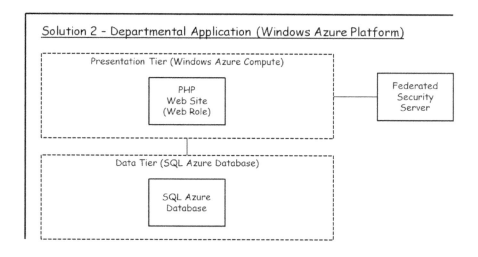

3 OPERATIONAL COST ANALYSIS

The dynamics and behaviors of some on-premise applications can be contrary to cost-effective operation in Windows Azure unless you make some changes. It's possible for a reasonable, well-written enterprise application to display unpleasant billing tendencies after being migrated to the cloud. This simply reflects that the basis for cost in the cloud is quite different from in the enterprise: enterprise applications were not designed with cloud computing in mind. For example, an inefficient application that does more communication than it needs to may not be noticed at all on-premise but this spurious activity could easily increase your Windows Azure bill. Even worse than higher-than-necessary costs are increasing costs, where an application costs you more month over month.

It's in your interest to discover and correct such situations as part of the migration process rather than being surprised by the size of your bills after deployment. Once you've tentatively mapped a solution's tiers and components to the Windows Azure platform, you should take a step back and think about whether it is a good fit for the pricing model of the cloud services you will be using.

1. Review your solution for indicators of possible high cost.
2. Determine what changes if any are required to your solution design and migration approach.
3. Check that your prior conclusions about migration cost, operating cost, and ROI are still valid based on what you have learned and how your plans have been revised.

Locating Cost Concern Points

In order to locate possible concern points in your solution you first need to be well-acquainted with the metering methods of each platform service you plan to use. Metering methods vary greatly from service to service and a number of services have more than one basis for charges. For example, Windows Azure Storage charges are based on 3 meters: storage size, storage transactions, and bandwidth. The pricing model is explained in Chapter 3, *Billing*, and also on Azure.com.

Excessive, Repetitive or Unnecessary Service Consumption

Think through how you expect your solution to consume the Windows Azure platform services. Focus on how charges are metered and when and where you invoke the service to incur charges. Is each instance of consumption necessary? Can some be eliminated, combined, or performed less frequently?

BEST PRACTICE: Avoid chatty or redundant consumption of cloud services unless there is a specific application justification for doing so.

Forgetting to Deallocate Resources

Resources left in the cloud that are not released cost you on an ongoing basis, month after month. This includes data as well as compute instances.

Historically, this is very similar to a classic problem programmers had with the C++ language in its heyday: it was easy to allocate memory and forget to deallocate it. "Memory leaks" were a common plague. The ballooning use of memory, while not noticed at first, eventually used up available resources and caused crashes. By the time the pain was felt the problems were well-entrenched. In the case of cloud computing, failing to deallocate resources is particularly painful as it results in a larger bill.

The best defense against the forgotten deallocation problem is to get disciplined about it. Whenever a resource is allocated, some mechanism should be in place to drive it getting deallocated at some point. It doesn't matter if these resources are allocated and deallocated programmatically or by administrators following a process as long as it gets done reliably at the right time.

BEST PRACTICE: If you allocate resources, ensure there is an automatic means of deallocating them when no longer needed (whether programmatically or through a process).

Missed Opportunities for Caching

Caching is keeping local copies of retrieved data for a short period of time so that you don't have to keep going back to get it. For example, most web browsers cache images so they don't have to keep pulling down the same image over and over in a session as you browse a web site. The use of caching can replace multiple invocations of a service with one invocation. Look for opportunities for your applications to cache results from cloud services for re-use. Think carefully about how long you should cache results and whether they should be tied to a user session.

Expensive Looping on Cloud Services

Tight loops that invoke a service can turn tiny fees in large bills. In particular there is a danger when you are looping to check for new data: those checks may incur a transaction fee and/or bandwidth charges, even if no data is retrieved or the data being checked for does not exist. For example, it would be a poor idea to access Windows Azure Storage in a tight code loop that polls a queue, checks for the existence of blobs, or queries table records repeatedly. These activities may be innocent in the enterprise but they can be costly in the cloud

Not Using the Best Alternative

Sometimes an approach in the cloud that most closely fits an enterprise approach isn't the most cost-effective choice. A common example is migration of a SQL

Server database, where the default migration approach is to move it to a SQL Azure database. This is often the right thing to do, but if the data access needs are simple another option to consider is Windows Azure Table Storage, which is significantly less expensive. To determine whether this actually makes sense you need to consider the data access features needed, the difference in operating costs, and the additional development time. If you don't consider all of your options, you may be picking a more expensive path than you need to.

Revising Your Design and Approach

If you've found areas of cost concern in your solution, your development group will need to figure out what design or implementation changes are necessary to avoid the unwanted behavior. Be sure to consider alternatives. Here are some examples of unwanted cost behavior and how they can be resolved.

Unwanted Behavior	Resolution
An application polls a queue in a tight loop. If migrated to Windows Azure, this behavior would result in high Windows Azure Storage transaction costs.	Change the code to adapt the time interval between polls based on how busy the queue has been lately. An idle queue gets polled less frequently than a busy queue.
An application leaves old data behind. If migrated to Windows Azure, this behavior would cause increasing storage charges over time.	Augment the application to recognize and flag older data. Put a process in place to periodically archive and delete older data from Production.
A web application reads images out of file storage then serves them up. If migrated to Windows Azure and the images are put in blob storage, this is unnecessary overhead and expense.	Take advantage of publicly-accessible blob storage and simply refer to blobs in web pages—allowing the user's browser to get the images directly. Taking the web site out of the way in image serving reduces overhead and expense.

Confirming Cost and ROI Expectations

Once you believe your migration approach is properly accounting for cost factors, perform a sanity check on operational cost. You may have previously made a tentative analysis of Total Cost of Ownership and Return on Investment but the above activities may have changed the picture, especially if you've had to make design changes based on cost considerations. Calculate the solution's TCO and ROI using the methods described in Chapter 9. Compare them to previous expectations and ensure prior conclusions are still valid.

In the example scenarios we've been considering, one cost concern is identified for Solution 1 and none for Solution 2.

Solution 1: Company Web Site Cost Concerns

Cost Concern	Resolution
ASP.NET uses SQL Server session state. If migrated to SQL Azure session state, there is no SQL Agent equivalent to remove old session records. This would cause data to balloon over time and increase costs.	Add a background service to the solution that will periodically clean up old records from the SQL Azure session state database.

4 ESTIMATING TASKS

For task estimation, you must identify the tasks needed to implement your mapping, as well as the various tasks that should be part of any software project such as design and stabilization. Here's a checklist for services to consider:

Preparation Tasks

☐ Architecture/Design, Security/Design
☐ Analysis/Research
☐ Migration and DR planning

Migration Tasks

☐ Code migration
☐ Database migration
☐ Database partitioning
☐ Non-database data migration
☐ Data movement
☐ Integration migration
☐ Security migration
☐ Instrument for activity monitoring and diagnostics
☐ Synchronization between cloud and on-premise
☐ *New Scope*

Completion Tasks

☐ QA
☐ Load testing
☐ Governance/monitoring/support

For a pilot or proof-of-concept, it isn't necessary to cover all of the preparation and completion tasks to the same extent you would for a formal implementation. This gives you the leeway to keep costs lower until you have proven out the validity of the approach.

Your estimate should not include unnecessary activities. Consider specifying a range of hours: use the high range to include recommended but optional tasks such as governance work. Ensure the low range includes all essential tasks.

TIP: On a first project, don't forget to budget time for learning curve and experimentation.

It's often easiest to think of these activities as each requiring some number of weeks. Here are task breakdowns for the example solutions we've been using:

Solution 1: Departmental Application Migration Tasks

Area	Task	Hours
Design	Architecture & Security Design	8
Code	Convert ASP.NET web site to Windows Azure Compute web role	8
Code	Convert WCF web services to Windows Azure Compute web role	8
Data	Convert SQL Server 2008 database to SQL Azure Database	8
Data	Migrate data to new database	8
Stabilization	Testing and debugging	40
Stabilization	Load testing and optimization	40
Total		**120**

Solution 2: Departmental Application Migration Tasks

Area	Task	Hours
Design	Architecture & Security Design	8
Code	Convert PHP web site to Windows Azure Compute web role	8
Data	Convert MySQL database to SQL Azure Database	16
Data	Migrate data to new database	8
Security	Install, configure, and integrate Federated Security Server in DMZ	40
Stabilization	Testing and debugging	40
Stabilization	Load testing and optimization	40
Total		**160**

If a migration is combined with adding new scope to a solution, it's a good idea to track costs separately. Migration costs should factor into your calculation of ROI but new scope work should not.

Cost Considerations

Development work is usually the primary expense in a migration but there can be other costs involved. The table below lists potential sources of migration expense.

Sources of Migration Expense

Source of Expense	Example
Development Work	Migrate code and data to Windows Azure
Software Licensing	New licenses must be purchased for third-party controls running in the cloud
Synchronization	New development / IT work to create synchronization of cloud and on-premise databases
Operations Monitoring	Integrating solution with Microsoft System Center
Compliance	Demonstrating cloud solution is HIPAA compliant
Corporate Review	Undergoing a review by our risk management group
Training	Training of IT and Development personnel on cloud

CHAPTER SUMMARY

In this chapter we presented a process for planning and estimating migrations of existing solutions to Windows Azure. This should include analyzing a solution to understand its composition, technology dependencies, and environment; mapping each to the cloud; analyzing operational costs; scoping the level of work involved; and estimating specific development tasks.

9

CALCULATING
TCO & ROI

"Wherein will that profit me?"
—*Aristophanes, The Clouds, 419 B.C.*

Whether or not cost reduction is your motivation for using cloud computing you certainly want to know what to expect financially from the Windows Azure Platform. Once you have a candidate solution in view you can calculate Total Cost of Ownership, Savings, and Return on Investment (if you have collected sufficient information). If you have skilled financial people at your disposal you should consider involving them in your analysis. In this chapter we present simple but revealing analyses anyone can perform that help you see the financial picture. We'll answer these questions:

- How is TCO calculated for a Windows Azure solution?
- How is savings determined?
- How is ROI calculated?

DEFINITIONS

To avoid confusion, let's clearly define what we will seek to calculate:

- *In-Cloud TCO*: cost of operating your solution on Windows Azure
- *On-Premise TCO*: cost of operating your solution on-premise or hosted
- *Savings*: the savings realized by moving a solution to the cloud
- *ROI*: the return on investment in moving a solution to the cloud

For a new cloud application, only In-Cloud TCO can be calculated. For existing solutions that are to be migrated, all of these values can be calculated.

TOTAL COST OF OWNERSHIP (TCO)

The concept behind TCO is illuminating what your full costs are: it's meant to account for both the direct and indirect costs of using a product or service. TCO is a noble idea but it can be tough to know if you've really taken everything into account. We're going to focus in this chapter on the *operational costs* of applications.

There are 2 kinds of TCO we may be able to calculate: *In-Cloud TCO* and *On-Premise TCO*.

- *In-Cloud TCO* is the cost of operating your solution on the Windows Azure platform. This value can be computed for new and migrated solutions.
- *On-Premise TCO* is the cost of operating your solution on-premise or with a traditional hosting provider. This value only has meaning for migrated solutions.

Since cloud computing costs are typically defined in terms of monthly charges, it makes sense to normalize both kinds of TCO and show them in monthly terms, allowing easy comparison.

Computing On-Premise TCO

On-premise TCO is sometimes difficult to compute, but doing so is certainly worthwhile if you are looking to justify a move to Windows Azure financially. If you happen to use traditional hosting or outsource some of your IT services you may have the convenience of a single bill that accounts for most of your costs. Otherwise, it's necessary to collect a variety of expense information. Below are categories of expense you should obtain data for if they apply. First obtain the figures in their natural form, which might be a monthly cost, an annual cost, or a one-time cost. Then normalize the expense by converting it to a monthly cost.

Type of Expense	Cost / Period	Monthly Cost
Hosting		
Facilities*		
Hardware		
Licensing		
Maintenance		
Labor		
Other		
Total		

* Facilities includes energy and cooling costs

To make TCO comparisons eminently fair, only include going-forward costs in the On-Premise TCO calculation. Don't worry about past investments such as hardware and software purchases. However, do include estimates of what you will spend on future hardware and software upgrades.

On the next page is an example of an On-Premise TCO calculation.

DOWNLOAD: You can download a worksheet for tracking TCO and ROI from http://-AzureHandbook.com (specify download code 145657471X).

Health Access Plus – On-Premise TCO

Type of Expense	Cost / Period	Monthly Cost
Hosting	$140,000 / year traditional hosting	$11,666
Facilities*		
Hardware		
Licensing	$9,600 in upgrades over next 4 years	$200
Maintenance		
Labor	$2,400 / year (3% of IT worker salary)	$200
Other		
Total		**$12,066**

Sometimes calculating TCO for a single application is a challenge because there are many shared resources used by more than one application. In particular, virtualization complicates matters as your application may be one of many running on shared hardware. If you cannot determine TCO at the application level, the next best thing is to estimate your overall IT TCO and take a percentage of that figure as belonging to the application you are analyzing. For example, "Our HR Benefits Portal is about 5% of our IT". While this will only produce a rough figure, it will give you something to use in a TCO comparison. Naturally the more complete and accurate your methods of estimation are, the more confidence you can place in your calculations and conclusions.

Calculating In-Cloud TCO

To compute TCO in the cloud you need to consider which services of the Windows Azure platform you plan to use and estimate your monthly consumption.

Windows Azure Monthly Charges Worksheet

Service / Monthly Rates*	Monthly Consumption	Monthly Charges
Data Transfers (Bandwidth) $0.10 GB / $0.15 GB out		
Windows Azure Compute Hourly: $0.05-$0.96/hour x instances		
Windows Azure Storage Size: $0.15 / GB Transactions: $0.01 / 10,000 tx		
Windows Azure CDN Bandwidth: $0.15 GB in / $0.15 GB out Transactions: $0.01 / 10,000 tx		
SQL Azure Database Size: $9.99 / GB x 1/5/10/20/30/40/50		
AppFabric Access Control Transactions: $1.99 per 100,000 tx		
AppFabric Service Bus Connections: $3.99 each or buy packs		
DataMarket Terms are specific to your subscription		
Other Other services / sources of expense		
Total		

* U.S. rates as of this writing. Check latest rates for your subscription and geo-location at Azure.com.

On the next page is an example In-Cloud TCO calculation.

Useful online tools for computing Windows Azure in-cloud TCO are:

- Microsoft's Windows Azure Platform TCO Calculator
  http://www.microsoft.com/windowsazure/economics/
- Neudesic's Azure ROI Calculator
  http://azureroi.cloudapp.net/

Be careful to work with the cloud mindset and not the enterprise mindset in estimating your costs. In the traditional enterprise model of buying server hardware in advance, you have to predict your peak use and purchase enough iron to support that load. In essence, <u>peak load</u> determines the size of your deployment and your costs. In the cloud, you have the benefit of elasticity where you can expand or reduce your deployment any time. Therefore, you should be modeling <u>average load</u> in your cost estimates.

Example of Estimated Windows Azure Monthly Charges

Service / Monthly Rates	Monthly Consumption	Monthly Charges
Data Transfers (Bandwidth) $0.10 GB / $0.15 GB out	750 GB in, 990 GB out	$75 + $149
Windows Azure Compute Hourly: $0.05-$0.96/hour x instances	4 servers, Small size VM	$351
Windows Azure Storage Size: $0.15 / GB Transactions: $0.01 / 10,000 tx	800 GB 15,000 tx / month	$120 + $0.02
Windows Azure CDN Bandwidth: $0.15 GB in / $0.15 GB out Transactions: $0.01 / 10,000 tx		
SQL Azure Database Size: $9.99 / GB x 1/5/10/20/30/40/50	2 x 50GB databases	$992
AppFabric Access Control Transactions: $1.99 per 100,000 tx	100,000 transactions	$1.99
AppFabric Service Bus Connections: $3.99 each or buy packs	25	$49.75
DataMarket Terms are specific to your subscription		
Other Other services / sources of expense		
Total		**$1,739**

SAVINGS

Your migration to the cloud will yield a difference in operating costs which in most cases will reflect a savings. Savings is simply the difference between your current operating costs and projected operating costs in the cloud. This is best expressed in monthly terms.

$$MonthlySavings = InCloudTCO - OnPremTCO$$

Once it is established that there will be savings in the cloud, the savings figure can be multiplied by the expected remaining lifetime of the application to determine total expected savings.

$$TotalSavings = Savings \times Months$$

Of course, savings doesn't take into account your cost of getting into the cloud. The ROI calculation does that.

RETURN ON INVESTMENT (ROI)

An ROI calculation indicates the gain you are expected to realize in moving to the Windows Azure platform. The ROI is determined by taking the savings you will realize over the lifetime of the application and subtracting from it the expense involved in getting into the cloud.

```
ROI = TotalSavings - MigrationExpenses
```

In order to compute ROI you need to know your total savings, which in turn means you have determined your in-cloud TCO, on-prem TCO, and projected application lifetime. You also need to know your migration expenses (as described in Chapter 8). You can't perform the ROI calculation unless you have all of these.

Monthly View of ROI

One valuable view of ROI is to plot monthly expenses, where you can show on-premise costs, in-cloud costs, and migration costs together. Be sure all understand that the on-prem and in-cloud costs are ongoing for as long as the application lives there, while the migration expenses are one-time in nature.

In the example monthly ROI view shown below, an application that cost $12,066 to run each month on-premise is being migrated to the Windows Azure platform where monthly costs are projected to be about $1,750—a savings of over $10,000 each month. The migration to the cloud will cost $54,000 over a 4-month period, and during that time the on-premise solution will continue to be operated. The monthly ROI view shows all of this clearly.

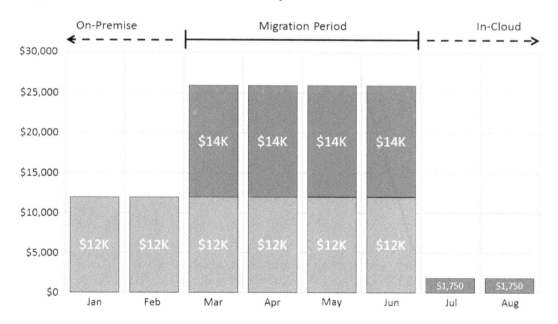

Lifetime View of ROI

Looking only at the first year of ROI can be very misleading, because the first year has the hit of one-time migration expenses while subsequent years do not. A second valuable view of ROI is over the expected remaining lifetime of the application. The lifetime ROI view below shows the same scenario from the previous section over an expected 5 years of life. Considering the lifetime of the application, the total ROI is a whopping $521,619!

CHAPTER SUMMARY

In this chapter we provided guidance on how to perform basic calculations of on-premise TCO, in-cloud TCO, savings, and ROI. Except for in-cloud TCO, these values only have meaning in the context of a migration where you are comparing on-premise costs to in-cloud costs. We looked at examples of TCO and ROI and explored various graphical ways to present ROI clearly.

10

ADOPTION STRATEGIES

"Vision is the art of seeing what is invisible to others."
—*Jonathan Swift*

Whether your use of Windows Azure is light or extensive, you should certainly be using it for well-defined reasons. A technology wave as big as cloud computing can be a game-changer for many organizations and is worth evaluating as a strategic tool. In this chapter we help you consider the possibilities by reviewing different ways in which Windows Azure can be used strategically by organizations. We also consider the impact it can have on your culture. We'll answer these questions:

- Are there different levels of adoption for Windows Azure?
- How can Windows Azure be strategically used by IT?
- How can Windows Azure affect your culture?
- How can Windows Azure further your business strategy?

LEVELS OF ADOPTION

There are different levels of adoption you can reach with Windows Azure as shown below. This is not meant as a maturity model per se, simply a way to show that organizations can reach deeper and deeper levels of immersion in cloud computing—to the point where it is not merely *valuable* but *strategic*.

1. Basic: used casually or peripherally
2. Core: an essential technology for IT
3. Transformative: transforms your IT culture and styles of computing
4. Strategic: an enabler for your business strategy

Windows Azure Levels of Adoption

VALUABLE -- STRATEGIC

1	2	3	4
Basic	**Core**	**Transformative**	**Strategic**
used casually / peripherally	an essential technology for IT	transforms IT culture / styles of computing	an enabler for your business strategy

1 BASIC ADOPTION

At the basic level of adoption you are using Windows Azure casually, occasionally, or experimentally. It's providing value, but is not central to your operations.

Here are some usage examples of basic adoption:

- Creating a public web site quickly for a temporary marketing campaign.
- Placing data in the cloud for clients to download
- Storing data in the cloud aggregated from multiple departments or organizations, none of whom want to host it themselves.
- An individual or department using cloud computing to get around delays or obstacles in going through normal IT channels.

As you have more and more positive experiences with Windows Azure and see its value firsthand, your usage and confidence in the platform will grow. When you start to use Windows Azure for mission-critical purposes you will have moved to the next level, core adoption.

2 CORE ADOPTION

At the core level of adoption Windows Azure has moved to center stage and is an essential technology that you depend on. It plays a major role in your IT operations. There are many value propositions to consider that might make Windows Azure worthy of playing a key role:

IT Value Propositions

Provisioning Strategies

Service Level

Data Center Strategies

IT Reduction Objectives

Outsourcing Aspects of IT

B2B Integration

Labor Efficiency and Realignment

Universal Access

Neutral Location

New Capabilities

Public-Private-Hybrid Cloud Strategy

If your organization has formal practices for handling governance, risk management, and compliance (GRC), integrating Windows Azure into them should be a top priority in core adoption.

Provisioning Strategies

Provisioning is a major function of IT and one that is often the hold-up in getting new IT initiatives off the ground. Windows Azure can have a substantial impact on the speed and nature of provisioning.

- *Rapid Provisioning*. In many companies procurement of IT assets takes a very long time: 6 weeks to 6 months is not uncommon. Windows Azure's ability to allocate IT assets in 20 minutes or less is lightning-fast in comparison.
- *Streamlined Provisioning,* The provisioning process can also be bureaucratic, complicated, or highly dependent on other people. With Windows Azure it's simple.
- *Self-Service Provisioning*. Not all organizations will warm to this idea, but for some it will be attractive to permit more self-service provisioning throughout the company. Windows Azure enables this scenario.
- *Client Provisioning*. Provisioning new clients can involve a multitude of activities; in some organizations this includes procuring, configuring, and deploying new IT resources. For the reasons mentioned above, the IT aspects of client provisioning can become rapid and streamlined with Windows Azure—delivering a better on-boarding experience for your customers.

Service Level

Service Level expectations and requirements vary by company and solution. Consider whether the Windows Azure SLA is an improvement over what your on-premise environment offers. The Windows Azure Compute SLA is 3½ 9's (99.95%) and the other platform services generally offer an SLA of 3 9's (99.9%).

Data Center Strategies

How you view your data center can be quite different when cloud computing is part of the mix.

- *Overflow*. You can use Windows Azure to handle overflow when your primary data center is overloaded.
- *Backup*. You can back up data to Windows Azure for safekeeping, where it is stored with triple redundancy.
- *Disaster Recovery*. You can fail over to Windows Azure in the event of a disaster with your own data center.
- *Plan for Average Load*. You can plan your data center for average load rather than peak load and use Windows Azure to make up the difference.
- *Deferring Upgrades*. You may be able to defer the expense of data center upgrades by routing new work to Windows Azure.

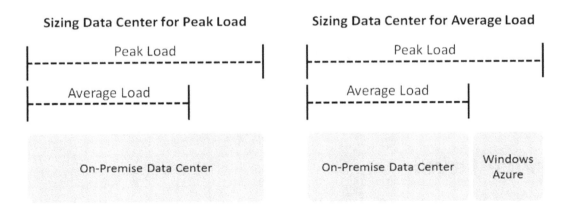

IT Reduction Objectives

Many companies have objectives in place to limit, freeze, or reduce data center size and IT spending. Windows Azure may be able to help you achieve those objectives or give you a means to add capacity without violating them.

- *Shift Assets Off-Premise.* Shifting some of your IT assets off-premise may allow you to meet cost reduction goals without sacrificing capacity.
- *Quietly Expand.* If you need more capacity but are barred from procuring new hardware or making new capital expenditures, Windows Azure may allow you get what you need when other doors are closed to you.

Outsourcing Aspects of IT

Not all companies do IT well and some would prefer not have to handle the difficult problems of building and maintaining scalable, reliable, highly available systems themselves. Since these qualities come with the use of Windows Azure automatically, outsourcing aspects of IT allows companies to focus more of their attention on their business. Windows Azure provides fast and simple provisioning, automatic patching, and health monitoring.

B2B Integration

Business-to-Business electronic integration with customers, partners, or suppliers is a complex area often requiring custom infrastructure or development work and individualized attention. Windows Azure has ground-breaking services that can help in this area:

- *AppFabric Service Bus* provides a publish-subscribe communication facility that is superb at navigating NATs, firewalls, and proxies. No special infrastructure changes are necessary for it work, not even opening a port.
- *AppFabric Access Control Service* supports the world's identity schemes and can federate them. With security implementation decoupled from application code, supporting new security schemes becomes a simpler, configuration-oriented process.

Labor Efficiency and Realignment

Certain IT tasks are performed automatically by Windows Azure that previously required the attention of IT workers. With a sufficient level of adoption this could have an effect on the size and make-up of your IT staff.

- *Do more with less.* Cloud computing may permit you to get more accomplished with fewer staff.
- *Focus IT workers on higher-level activities.* With Windows Azure taking care of many low-level details there is an opportunity to refocus IT personnel on higher level work—in effect, taking everyone's job up a notch.

Universal Access

Some on-premise applications are difficult for all users to reach. Applications requiring a VPN connection are one example, where distance or being at a field location might degrade or altogether prevent employees from being able to use the application. Putting applications and data in the cloud gives you systems that are universally accessible (and can still be secured).

Neutral Location

Occasionally it is politically expedient to put applications or data in a neutral location rather than at one organization or another. For example, an industry exchange might be adopted more strongly if it was distanced from a member company's domain. Windows Azure is a perfect choice for a "Switzerland" location that can be easily accessed by all without playing favorites.

New Capabilities

Some capabilities provided by Windows Azure are compelling and simply don't exist elsewhere.

- *DataMarket:* subscription-based reference data
- *Service Bus*: firewall-friendly publish-subscribe communication
- *Access Control Service*: federated security with broad interoperability

Public-Private-Hybrid Cloud Strategy

Public cloud computing is in full swing, and the technology industry is quickly innovating to deliver on the concepts of *private cloud* and *hybrid cloud*—in response to great levels of market interest. Before going further, we'd better define these terms.

Example of Public, Private, and Hybrid Clouds

Public Cloud	Private Cloud	Hybrid Cloud
Windows Azure		Windows Azure
	Hyper-V	Hyper-V

Public Cloud

Public cloud is the use of computing services from a technology provider who operates their own data centers that support dynamic allocation and mammoth scale. The Windows Azure platform is a public cloud.

Private Cloud

The concept of *private cloud* seems simple enough at first—"I want cloud computing capabilities, but privately or locally." In fact, there are at least 6 different meanings people attach to this term! Let's review them:

1. *Hardware Private Cloud* refers to a hardware appliance that provides similar capabilities to a public cloud data center. These can be expensive! Microsoft has announced a Windows Azure Appliance is coming but availability and pricing are not known as of this writing.

2. *Software Private Cloud* is a software emulation of what a public cloud does without the specialized infrastructure. In the Windows Azure world we do not have this today but there are some forerunners: There is a single-machine Windows Azure Simulation Environment that developers can use today. The convergence of Windows Server AppFabric and Windows Azure AppFabric may also yield some capability in this area.

3. *Network Private Cloud* involves connecting your assets in the cloud and your on-premise assets with a virtual network (VPN) connection. This more properly belongs in the next category, *Hybrid Cloud*.

4. *Dedicated Private Cloud*. This means an area of a public cloud has been put aside just for your company instead of the usual isolated-but-shared-resource arrangement, at a higher price of course. Microsoft has offered this for some of its online cloud services such as BPOS ("BPOS-D") but not for Windows Azure.

5. *Enterprise Virtualization*. Some people refer to their use of virtualization in the enterprise as a private cloud. Today a purist might disagree that enterprise virtualization qualifies as cloud computing, but as virtualization products develop more capabilities found in public cloud this will become a more and more appropriate designation.

6. *Local Network*. This is not a very good use of the term "cloud" but it's what some people mean by "private cloud".

Hybrid Cloud

Hybrid cloud is the idea of connecting your public cloud with your private cloud (if you have one) or your local network. This can be achieved with VPN technology such as Windows Azure Connect, and can range from mere network connections to domain joining and authentication. Hybrid cloud allows you to place assets in the cloud while still allowing them to work closely with on-premise systems and management tools.

Multi-Cloud Strategies

Depending on existing investments and interests, you might find yourself getting exposed to public cloud before private cloud or vice-versa. Either way, the time will come when you'll need to ask some questions about which of these forms of cloud computing you want to use, for what reasons, and whether there is interaction between them. Here are some different decisions that organizations arrive at:

- *No Cloud.* It's possible to opt out of the cloud phenomenon altogether, though rare. Like virtualization and devices, the benefits of cloud computing are too good to ignore.
- *Enterprise-centric, Elective use of Cloud.* Here you default to deploying applications and data in the enterprise but make elective decisions from time to time to use the cloud when it is justified on a case-by-case basis.
- *Cloud-centric, Elective use of Enterprise.* Here you default to the cloud but occasionally choose to use the enterprise when justified.
- *Well-defined Roles for Cloud and Enterprise.* Here you have clearly defined what belongs in the cloud and what belongs in the enterprise and issued guidance about how to make this determination.
- *Problem applications go in the cloud.* If you have "problem applications" that don't fit into your data center well for technical or policy reasons, running them in the cloud may be an acceptable alternative.
- *All in Cloud.* Everything you do is in the public cloud. This is not a viable goal for most established businesses, at least not in the near term, but it is popular with start-ups (see *Zero Local IT* later in this chapter).

3 TRANSFORMATIVE ADOPTION

In the transformative level of adoption your corporate culture is being affected, both inside and outside of the IT department. Windows Azure has become more than an essential technology: it has changed your approach to solving IT problems and introduced new styles of computing. You have made a deep commitment to the platform and its use is assumed and taken for granted.

Transformational Effects

New Styles of Computing

Zero Local IT

Affordable Experimentation and Innovation

Democratization of IT / Self-Service IT

New Styles of Computing

Windows Azure enables new styles of computing not previously available or not practical in the enterprise.

Burst Computing

In burst computing you operate in an on-demand world, allocating resources at the moment you need them and releasing them as soon as you are done with them.

For example, imagine you have a batch process that runs at the end of each month, taking 24 hours to complete on a server. Your colleagues are very interested in getting the results as soon as possible and you would like to turn them around faster. With some changes to your application, you can go from running 24 hours on 1 local server to running in 1 hour on 24 servers in the cloud, which only costs you for the 60 minutes.

Self-Scaling & Self-Terminating Applications

Applications can be written to monitor their own activity and scale themselves larger or smaller automatically in response to workload. You can also write applications that terminate themselves and their data when no longer needed. Self-scaling and self-terminating applications are valuable because they take away the need for human beings to watch over them and manage or remove them. Applications that size themselves and shut down when finished save you money.

Grid Computing

Grid computing allows you to attack problems with massive parallelism. Grid computing was once limited to specific industries and problem scenarios such as actuarial analysis and human genome processing, and used to require either a large standing army of machines or use "cycle stealing" to repurpose computers during off-hours for problem-solving. Using cloud computing as a foundation, grid computing can now be performed very economically, without a data center investment, and is therefore suited for a much broader collection of scenarios including smaller-scale uses. Examples are data analysis, modeling and simulation, image recognition, and real-time processing such as fraud detection. While grid computing is not an out-of-box feature of Windows Azure, the platform provides 95% of what is needed in a grid computing environment.

Here's an example of a business grid computing application. A large-scale headhunting service has many incoming resumes that need to be quickly matched to available job openings to ascertain the best matches. Each received resume is scanned and queued as a resume comparison task. The grid computing network performs these tasks with massive parallelism, and from the resulting scores the top matches can be pursued by recruiters.

Hybrid Applications

Hybrid applications—partially on-premise and partially in the cloud—are gaining in popularity. A consumer example would be Apple's iTunes or Microsoft's Zune: there is local software you install locally on your computer coupled with a music store "out in the cloud". This approach makes sense for certain business scenarios.

An example of a business hybrid application is a CRM solution where the front end is a locally-installed desktop application (to allow for disconnected operation) coupled with a cloud-hosted server application.

Zero Local IT

Some companies embrace the idea of "Zero Local IT", where *everything* is in the cloud except user devices (computers, phones, etc.). This notion is especially popular with start-up companies. To achieve Zero Local IT with the Microsoft platform, consider using not only Windows Azure (to run your own applications) but also Office 365 (Office, Exchange Online, SharePoint Online, Lync) and CRM Online to support your operations.

Affordable Experimentation & Innovation

You can promote greater experimentation and innovation across your company when you are using Windows Azure because costs are lower and you can stop paying for resources when they are no longer felt to be justified. If you want to enable widespread entrepreneurial activity and empower self-directed research, Windows Azure is the way to do it affordably.

Democratization of IT / Self-Service IT

Windows Azure can be used to make some IT functions self-service such as provisioning, deployment, upgrades, and scaling—allowing departments or individuals to directly perform IT operations without having to go through the IT department. Some companies embrace this idea wholeheartedly, some resist it, and some are open to it. For companies that pursue the democratization of IT, there are several levels at which it can be offered:

- *Direct portal access.* You can give qualified individuals direct access to the Windows Azure portal (however, consider the security implications).
- *Custom portal.* You can create a custom portal using the Windows Azure Service Management API that permits a subset of management actions based on permissions you grant to users or departments.
- *Cloud-savvy applications.* You can build cloud computing concepts into your business applications and give your users control over aspects of resource allocation and cost. There are ways to do this in terms the user can relate to.

Here's an example of a cloud-savvy business application. Consider an application in which workers submit long-running jobs but have an option for requesting priority processing if they are willing to charge the extra cost to their department. The application processes standard jobs using a common VM farm in the cloud for which there is standing budget. For priority jobs new VMs are allocated to service those jobs right away, at added cost. In this example cloud computing concepts have been woven into the application to allow a speed-vs.-cost decision that is expressed to the user in terms they can relate to, not technical terms.

4 STRATEGIC ADOPTION

At the strategic level of adoption Windows Azure is an enabler for your business strategy. It has become a partner technology that furthers your business goals, fosters innovation, and helps you achieve a competitive edge.

Strategic Value Propositions

Using Disruption to Your Advantage

Financial Aid

Enabling New Business Models like SaaS

Leveling the Playing Field

Achieving Global Reach

Preserving the Option to Walk Away

A Better Service Level for Clients

Landing the Big Fish

Scaling Fast and Rapid Expansion

Planning for Uncertainty

Data Revenue

Using Disruption to Your Advantage

Cloud computing is often described as a *disruptive technology*, and it is: it upsets the applecart, bringing great benefit while challenging the status quo. The first level of disruption is internal and obvious: your organization will be impacted as it learns to leverage the technology properly and effectively.

The second level of disruption may be less obvious: you can turn Windows Azure into a business weapon to create disruption in your industry and markets, giving you an advantage. For example, you might be able to offer your products and services in forms or prices your competitors can't easily match.

Learning to commandeer technology disruption for your own benefit is kind of like seeing an incoming tidal wave as an opportunity to go surfing; it requires you to understand what's coming and climb on board instead of being overwhelmed by it or resisting it.

Financial Aid

The cost model in the cloud, vastly different from in the enterprise, can drastically reduce expenses, remove financial barriers, and enable business scenarios that would not otherwise make sense.

- *Reduced costs* are generally to be expected with cloud computing. For some organizations IT costs are reduced as much as ten-fold.
- *Converting CapEx to OpEx* is attractive to some organizations from an accounting standpoint and eliminates up-front hardware purchases.
- *Pay as you go pricing* allows you to have business initiatives whose IT expenses are closely aligned with their operational lifetimes and associated revenue flow.
- *On-demand computing* allows you to discard an IT asset the moment you no longer need it and stop paying for it.

Enabling New Business Models like SaaS

The cloud may put new business models in reach or improve the viability of existing ones. Consider *Software as a Service* which is best offered on a cloud computing platform. You benefit from the economy of a single deployment, and Windows Azure provides you the assurance of being able to scale to any level to keep pace with your growth no matter how successful you are.

Leveling the Playing Field

Windows Azure makes it possible for countries, organizations and individuals to have access to the world's finest data centers with a low cost of entry. This levels the playing field in many ways. From developing nations to small start-up businesses on a shoestring budget, it's now possible to compete on an even IT footing with anyone, anywhere.

Achieving Global Reach

Windows Azure can be a means of achieving global reach. With Microsoft's data centers and supporting infrastructure you can expand your presence to a worldwide level. It's just as easy and automatic to allocate resources halfway around the world as it is locally with Windows Azure.

Preserving the Option to Walk Away

If you need to preserve the option of quickly and cleanly terminating an IT initiative, there's no better way than with cloud computing. With a month-to-month subscription, you can walk away from Windows Azure any time with no obligations beyond your current month's bill. It's an easy-in, easy-out environment.

A Better Service Level for Clients

The reliable environment of Windows Azure guards the availability of your applications and the integrity of your data. Your clients will benefit from a better level of service.

Landing the Big Fish

Sometimes IT can be a catch-22 when you're pursuing new business: you may need to demonstrate a certain level of capability in order to win a deal, but you don't want to invest in that capability unless you know you have the deal. With a Windows Azure approach you can demonstrate you have access to a mammoth level of capacity on tap that is reliable, highly available, and expertly administered.

Scaling Fast and Rapid Expansion

Traditional IT doesn't have a reputation for being nimble, and this could lead to missed opportunities. You could receive a large amount of new business without warning, or want to seize an opportunity that requires an overnight response. With Windows Azure, you have on-demand computing at your disposal 24 x 7. You can have the IT resources you need within minutes of requesting them.

Imagine you've been keeping your data center fairly small until the time comes when you land that "big fish". When that time comes, you may suddenly need to scale up by an order of magnitude! With Windows Azure you can do so calmly, easily, and rapidly. By the same token, you can rapidly downsize when you need to. If that large customer goes away you don't want a major IT investment to go to waste or continue to cost you operating expenses. In the cloud, you simply dismiss what you no longer need and stop paying for it.

Planning for Uncertainty

In recent years, much has become uncertain. It's harder than ever to make long-term plans when you don't know what will happen to the economy, to your industry, and to your customers. Windows Azure is the safe bet when you're not sure how much IT you need or for how long: you only pay for what you use and only use what you need, without having to make any term or usage level commitments. It's a way to plan for uncertainty.

Data Revenue

You can sell data through the Windows Azure DataMarket service. If you have useful data you're willing to sell, Windows Azure can help you find "coins in the couch". You can sell data at proper value as you control the terms of sale.

CHAPTER SUMMARY

In this chapter we reviewed the various levels of adoption possible with Windows Azure: basic, core, transformational, and strategic. At the basic level usage is casual. At the core level the platform has become essential. At the transformation level you are committed to the cloud and it is affecting your culture and styles of computing. At the strategic level Windows Azure helps enable your business strategy.

APPENDIX A
WINDOWS AZURE RESOURCES

GENERAL

http://azure.com is the most important online resource for Windows Azure, and will link you to many other important online resources. Blogs from Microsoft and community members are also vital resources.

ASSESSMENT RESOURCES

Windows Azure Migration Assistance Tool (MAT) (Microsoft)
Available through Microsoft partners

Microsoft Cloud Computing Assessment (Neudesic)
http://cloud-assessment.com

Case Studies on Azure.com (Microsoft)
http://www.microsoft.com/windowsazure/evidence/

BILLING & PRICING RESOURCES

Microsoft Online Services Customer Portal (Billing Portal)

https://mocp.microsoftonline.com

Windows Azure Pricing Model (Microsoft)

http://www.microsoft.com/WindowsAzure/offers/

"What Will It Cost?" Example (Microsoft)

http://msdn.microsoft.com/en-us/library/ff803375.aspx

Windows Azure TCO Calculator (Microsoft)

http://www.microsoft.com/windowsazure/economics/

Azure ROI Calculator (Neudesic)

http://www.microsoft.com/windowsazure/economics/

COMMUNITY, EVENTS & NEWS

Windows Azure Forums on MSDN (Microsoft)

http://social.msdn.microsoft.com/Forums/en-US/category/windowsazureplatform

Azure User Group (community)

http://azureusergroup.com

Facebook: WindowsAzure

http://www.facebook.com/windowsazure

Twitter: @WindowsAzure

http://twitter.com/#!/WindowsAzure

Events on Azure.com (Microsoft)

http://www.microsoft.com/windowsazure/events/default.aspx

Announcements on Azure.com (Microsoft)

http://www.microsoft.com/windowsazure/announcements/default.aspx

Oakleaf Systems Blog (Roger Jennings)

http://oakleafblog.blogspot.com/

Microsoft MVPs for Windows Azure

https://mvp.support.microsoft.com/communities/mvp.aspx?product=1&competency=Windows+Azure&sortby=name

DEVELOPER RESOURCES

Windows Azure Developer Center (Microsoft)

http://msdn.microsoft.com/en-us/windowsazure

Online Documentation – Windows Azure (Microsoft)

http://msdn.microsoft.com/en-us/library/dd179367.aspx

Online Documentation – SQL Azure (Microsoft)

http://msdn.microsoft.com/en-us/library/ff937661.aspx

Online Documentation – AppFabric (Microsoft)

http://msdn.microsoft.com/en-us/library/gg577633.aspx

Windows Azure Design Patterns (David Pallmann)

http://azuredesignpatterns.com

Windows Azure Samples (David Pallmann)

http://azuresamples.com

MARKETPLACE

Windows Azure Marketplace for Data (Microsoft)

https://datamarket.azure.com/

Windows Azure Marketplace for Applications (Microsoft)

http://windowsazure.pinpoint.microsoft.com

PORTALS

Production Portals

Windows Azure Portal (Microsoft)

The primary portal, provides links to the other portals

http://windows.azure.com

SQL Azure Portal (Microsoft)

http://sql.azure.com

Billing Portal *see Billing and Pricing Resources*

AppFabric Portal (Microsoft)

https://appfabric.azure.com

Pre-Release Labs Portals

SQL Azure Labs Portal (Microsoft)

http://www.sqlazurelabs.com

AppFabric Labs Portal (Microsoft)

http://portal.appfabriclabs.com

SUPPORT

Billing, Subscription Management, and Quota Support (Microsoft)

https://mocp.microsoftonline.com/Site/Support.aspx

Windows Azure Technical Support (Microsoft)

http://www.microsoft.com/windowsazure/support/

Windows Azure Service Dashboard (Worldwide Service Status)

http://www.microsoft.com/windowsazure/support/status/servicedashboard.aspx

Windows Azure Feature Requests & Suggestions (Microsoft)

http://www.mygreatwindowsazureidea.com

TRAINING RESOURCES

Cloud Cover video show on Channel 9 (Microsoft)

http://channel9.msdn.com/Shows/Cloud+Cover

Windows Azure Bootcamp (Microsoft)

http://azurebootcamp.com

Windows Azure Platform Training Kit (Microsoft)

http://go.microsoft.com/fwlink/?LinkID=130354

APPENDIX B
GLOSSARY OF TERMS

Below are the definitions of terms used frequently in the text.

API	Application Programming Interface: a service or library for programmers.
Assessment	A process for envisioning risk & reward, analyzing opportunities, and strategizing.
Authentication	Determining the identity of a user or client program.
Authorization	Determining the permissions to grant a user or client program.
Bandwidth	The data rate a network or interface is able to support.
Blob	Binary Large Object: file-like data, a named series of bytes.
CapEx	Capital expenditures: money spent to acquire or upgrade physical assets.

Cloud service	A cloud-hosted application such as a web site or a web service.
Compliance	Conforming with stated requirements.
Container	Hardware: an ITPAC module in a data center. Software: a "folder" for blobs.
CTP	Community Technology Preview, early access to technologies before release.
DR	Disaster Recovery: analysis, readiness, and execution of recovering from a disaster.
Fault domain	A mechanism for spreading VMs across the data center to minimize disasters.
Firewall	Part of a network or computer system that blocks unauthorized access.
Governance	The mechanisms an organization uses to ensure established policies are followed.
GRC	A combined approach to Governance, Risk management, and Compliance.
HA	High Availability.
HTML	Hyper Text Markup Language, the principal markup language for web pages.
HTTP	Hyper Text Transfer Protocol, the communication protocol of the web.
HTTPS	Hyper Text Transfer Protocol Secure: HTTP over SSL.
Instance	One VM that is a member of a role (VM farm).
Latency	The delay incurred in processing network data.

Load balancer	An access point that accepts traffic and distributes it across a farm of servers.
Markup language	A <TAG>-based computer language (or notation), usually based on XML.
Migration	Moving from old to new, as in from on-premise to a cloud computing data center.
Mitigation	To lessen or make less severe.
Multi-tenant	Applications or services that serve multiple customers from a single deployment.
OData	A web protocol for querying and updating data, based on HTTP and AtomPub.
OpEx	Operational expenditures: money spent on ongoing business expenses.
Remote desktop	A way to access a remote computer that simulates using it directly.
REST	REpresentational State Transfer, a popular design for web-based services.
Risk management	The identification, assessment, prioritization, and mitigation of risks.
ROI	Return on Investment. Operational cost savings in the cloud minus migration costs.
Role	In Windows Azure, a container and design pattern for a farm of VM images.
RPO	Recovery Point Objective: in an SLA, how old data will be after disaster recovery.
RTO	Recovery Time Objective: in an SLA, how long it will take to recover from a disaster.
SLA	Service Level Agreement: an operations agreement between business and IT.

SSL	Secure Sockets Layer, a standard for encrypted, secure communication.
Table	A collection of structured data in the form of records or entities.
Threat model	An analysis of a threat showing vectors of attack and mitigations.
TCO	Total Cost of Ownership, a measure of total expenses (direct and indirect).
TDS	Tabular Data Stream, the protocol used by SQL Server and SQL Azure.
Upgrade domain	A mechanism for maintaining high availability while upgrading a cloud service.
Virtual network	A computer network that connects systems securely over the public Internet.
VM	Virtual Machine, a software-emulated computer that runs on a physical computer.
XML	eXtensible Markup Language, the leading markup language standard.

INDEX